The Education Center, Inc.'s

Back-To-School Book
From Your Friends At The Mailbox®

Grades K–5

Edited and compiled by:
Jennifer Overend

Edited by:
Amanda Wheeler
Kathy Wolf

Copyedited by:
Debbie Blaylock

Illustrated by:
Cathy Spangler Bruce

Cover design by:
Cathy Spangler Bruce

Typography by:
Lynette Maxwell

About This Book

Glide into the school year with the *Back-To-School Book From Your Friends At* The Mailbox®. This book provides hundreds and hundreds of teacher-tested activities contributed by subscribers of *The Mailbox*® magazine. Whether you're looking for bulletin-board ideas, getting-to-know-you activities, organizational tips, or thematic units, you'll find it all, plus much more, in this fantastic resource.

Table Of Contents

Registration Photos

With the help of a Polaroid camera, keep young children fascinated and occupied during registration. Snap a picture of each child and let him watch the photograph develop before his eyes. Collect the photographs from the children before they leave. Then write students' names on the pictures so you can match names and faces on the first day of school.

Mary Hanson—Gr. K, Murry Fly Elementary, Odessa, TX

Welcoming Phone Calls

Surprise students and parents before school starts with friendly phone greetings. Invite parents to attend Open House and tell students how much you look forward to having them in your class. These reassuring calls help students and parents feel more at ease with the coming school year.

Renee Myers—Gr. K, Snowville Elementary, Hiwassee, VA

A Friendly Hello

Help students and parents feel more comfortable about the new school year with personal letters. Mail the letters to the students' families before the beginning of school. In each letter, welcome the child to your class and share some of your personal information such as hobbies, interests, and family members. Invite parents to visit your class and to call you with any questions or concerns. Parents and students alike are sure to appreciate these friendly gestures.

Karen Cook—Gr. K, McDonough Primary School, McDonough, GA

Before-School Questionnaire

On your mark! Get set! Go! Get a head start learning about your students with this idea. Duplicate one copy of the questionnaire on page 4. Program the page with any necessary questions or information. Then duplicate copies for each child in your class. Mail a questionnaire to each child's parent several weeks before school begins. Encourage parents to return their questionnaires during the first week of school to provide you with valuable information about your students.

Christy Owens—Gr. K, West Alexandria Elementary, West Alexandria, OH

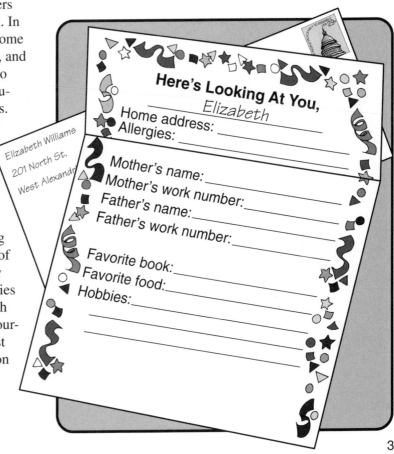

Elizabeth Williams
201 North St.
West Alexandr

Here's Looking At You, *Elizabeth*

Home address: _____
Allergies: _____

Mother's name: _____
Mother's work number: _____
Father's name: _____
Father's work number: _____

Favorite book: _____
Favorite food: _____
Hobbies: _____
_____
_____

Here's Looking At You,

_____

Note To Teacher: Use with "Before-School Questionnaire" on page 3.

Do Not Open!

To build on the natural anticipation children experience as a new year approaches, send each student a letter two weeks before school starts. On the back of the envelope, write in large letters "DO NOT OPEN UNTIL YOU WAKE UP ON THE FIRST DAY OF SCHOOL!" Inside the envelope, enclose a message describing the fun activities planned for the first day. Also include a half of a paper circle, cut in an unusual way, with instructions to bring it to school. When the children arrive on the first day with their half-circles, each is challenged to find the classmate with the matching half. What a fun way to begin a new year!

Jodi L. Tuskowski—Grs. 5–6, Madison Elementary, Stevens Point, WI

Back-To-School Pen Pals

Facilitate student friendships before the beginning of school by arranging pen pals. Several weeks before school starts, mail a welcome letter to each child in your class. In the letter, include the name and address of another student and encourage the child to write a letter to her. Be sure to give suggestions for information the child could share with her new pen pal. On the first day of school, have students locate their pen pals and meet face to face.

Dawn Warner—Gr. 2, Hebrew Academy Of Indianapolis, Indianapolis, IN

An Evening At School

Back-to-school jitters are set at ease with an evening at school. Plan to have an orientation night the week before school begins. Invite parents and their children to attend. Allow children and parents to investigate the areas of your classroom and ask questions. Inform parents of any supplies their children will need to bring to school. At the end of the evening, offer a short tour of the school for new students. Serve juice and cookies in the lunchroom and have each parent fill out an information card for his child. This pleasant evening together is a comfortable way for you, your students, and your students' parents to begin the school year.

Karen M. Hoffmeier—Gr. K, Thomas Jefferson School, Newton, IA

Welcome-Back Coloring Book

Generate back-to-school excitement with informative coloring books. A few weeks before school starts, duplicate pages 6 and 7. Program the necessary information; then duplicate copies for your students. Cut the pages apart and staple them into booklets. Mail a coloring book to each of your students. Students will enjoy receiving gifts from their new teacher, and parents will appreciate the helpful information.

Linda Patten—Gr. 3, Leary School, Rush, NY

5

Welcome To Grade _____

Coloring Book

©The Education Center, Inc. • TEC856

Your teacher's name is _____.

©The Education Center, Inc. • TEC856

Note To Teacher: Use with "Welcome-Back Coloring Book" on page 5.

This year we will learn about _____

_____

_____.

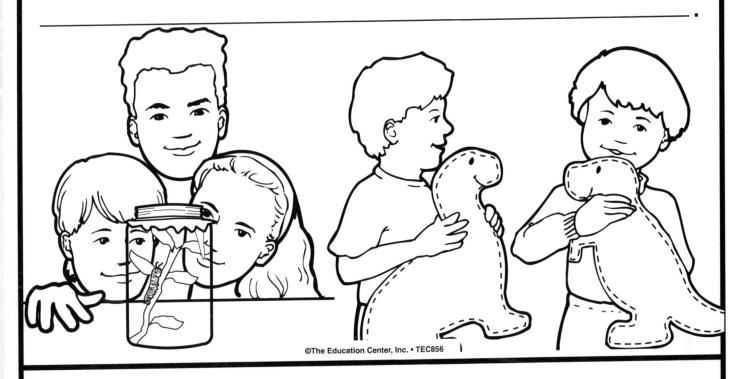

©The Education Center, Inc. • TEC856

You will need to bring the following items to school: _____

_____.

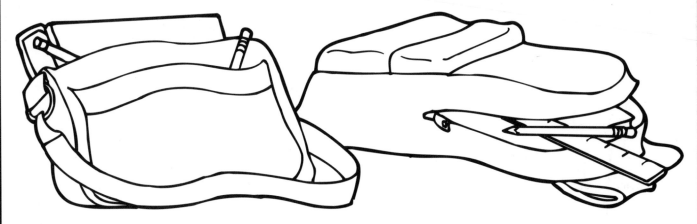

I'll see you soon!   Sincerely,

_____

©The Education Center, Inc. • TEC856

Student Information

These useful cards keep valuable student information at your fingertips. Duplicate an information card from page 11 for each of your students. Record the necessary information for each student and file the cards for future reference.

Cathy Armstrong—Gr. K, Bain Elementary School, Charlotte, NC

Computer Plans

Lesson planning at the beginning of the year can be a bit tricky, so try this helpful tip. A few weeks before school starts, record your preliminary plans and ideas on a computer. This allows you to change and reorganize your ideas quickly. Then, before the first day, finalize your plans, print out a copy, and clip it into your lesson-plan book.

Betty Adams—Gr. 5, Staunton Elementary School, Staunton, IN

Make A List!

The key to a hassle-free start to your year is organization. Duplicate the handy checklists on pages 9 and 10 to record your many tasks, meetings, and preparations during the first day and the first week of school.

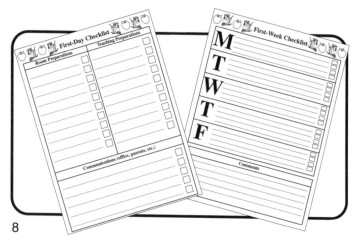

Class Schedule

Used as an information sheet or as a miniposter, this chart displays the days and times of your special classes. Duplicate a copy of page 12; then program the chart with the appropriate information. Store the chart inside your lesson-plan book or display it on a wall in your room.

First-Day Checklist

Room Preparations

☐
☐
☐
☐
☐
☐
☐
☐
☐
☐

Teaching Preparations

☐
☐
☐
☐
☐
☐
☐
☐
☐
☐

Communications (office, parents, etc.)

☐
☐
☐
☐
☐

Note To Teacher: Use with "Make A List" on page 8.

First-Week Checklist

M _____
_____
_____
_____

T _____
_____
_____
_____

W _____
_____
_____
_____

T _____
_____
_____
_____

F _____
_____
_____
_____

Comments

_____
_____
_____
_____
_____
_____

Note To Teacher: Use with "Make A List" on page 8.

Student Information Card

First name _____ Last name _____

Student no. _____

Address _____

City _____ State _____ Zip _____

Mother's name _____ Father's name _____ Home phone _____

Mother's work phone _____ Father's work phone _____ Student's birth date _____

Comments: _____

Medical concerns: _____

In an emergency, call: _____

Student Information Card

First name _____ Last name _____

Student no. _____

Address _____

City _____ State _____ Zip _____

Mother's name _____ Father's name _____ Home phone _____

Mother's work phone _____ Father's work phone _____ Student's birth date _____

Comments: _____

Medical concerns: _____

In an emergency, call: _____

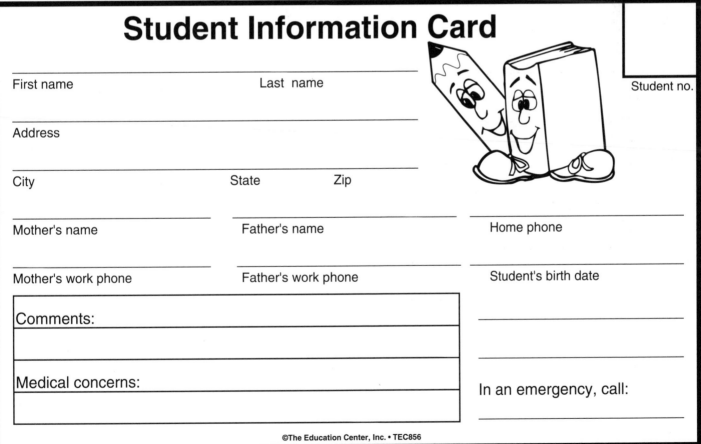

Note To Teacher: Use with "Student Information" on page 8.

teacher

grade

Special Class Schedule

Class		M	T	W	T	F
Music	Time:					
P.E.	Time:					
Library	Time:					
Art	Time:					
Computer	Time:					
	Time:					

Students attending other classes (speech, band, etc.): _____

_____

_____

Note To Teacher: Use with "Class Schedule" on page 8.

Photo Cards

These picturesque cards are helpful tools for your classroom. Photograph each child on the first day of school. Develop them quickly and have two copies made. Mount the photographs on 5" x 7" cards and use them for a variety of purposes.

Suggestions for use:

—Choose your daily class leader by drawing a different child's photo card each day.

—Form cooperative groups by randomly choosing two to four students' cards per group.

—Use photos later in the year to enclose with gifts to parents.

—Match names to faces with a fun game. Mount the photo cards on poster board. Make a small name strip for each child. Attach a piece of adhesive to the bottom of each photo. Then attach the opposite piece of Velcro to the back of the name strip. Have students match each name to the correct photo.

VaReane Gray Heese—Gr. 2, Omaha, NE
Kim Ennis—Gr. K, Smith's Station Primary School, Smiths, AL

Premier Plans

Your weekly plans will look truly impressive with these planning sheets. Duplicate a supply of pages 14 and 15. Keep them on hand throughout the year for recording your weekly plans.

All-In-One Notebook

Stay organized all year long with this convenient notebook system. Label a five-subject notebook with sections such as Things To Do, Faculty-Meeting Notes, Ideas, Classes, and Workshops. In these sections record important information, responsibilities, and ideas. Everything you need to remember is at your fingertips.

Therese Durhman—Gr. 5, Mountain View School, Hickory, NC

Seating Charts

Be prepared for substitute teachers by constructing your class seating chart. Duplicate your choice of page 16 or page 17. Label the spaces with your students' names and store the chart in your plan book.

Lesson plans for the week of _____

teacher _____   grade _____

Subject:		
Time:		

	Monday			
	Tuesday			
	Wednesday			
	Thursday			
	Friday			

©The Education Center, Inc. • TEC856

Note To Teacher: Use with "Premier Plans" on page 13.

Duty: ☐ A.M. _____ ☐ Noon _____ ☐ P.M. _____

			Monday	
			Tuesday	
			Wednesday	
			Thursday	
			Friday	

©The Education Center, Inc. • TEC856

Note To Teacher: Use with "Premier Plans" on page 13.

15

Seating Chart

Teacher: _____

Room No.: _____

Grade: _____

16

Note To Teacher: Use with "Seating Charts" on page 13.

Seating Chart

Teacher: _____

Room No.: _____

Grade: _____

Note To Teacher: Use with "Seating Charts" on page 13.

Job-Chart Clipboard

This durable chart can be used from year to year to help organize your classroom jobs.

Materials:
mat board or cardboard
poster board
paper cutter
scissors
adhesive labels
marker
cup hooks (one for each classroom job)
Formica samples with holes in the tops (one for each student)

Steps:
1. To make the clipboard, cut the mat board or cardboard to the desired size using a paper cutter. Then cut the clipboard shape from poster board and attach it as shown.
2. Write each class job on an adhesive label. Attach the labels in rows on the clipboard.
3. Screw in a cup hook (below each label).
4. Use a marker to label each Formica sample with a child's name. Store the samples near the chart.
5. Suspend the Formica samples from the cup hooks to show the students' weekly jobs. Change the Formica samples each week.

Sherri Nock—Gr. 3, Jupiter Farms Community School, Jupiter, FL

Teddy–Bear Helper Display

A large stuffed teddy bear can make an adorable display for your class jobs. Dress your bear in appropriately sized clothing. Attach pockets to the clothing, each labeled with a different class job. Then make small cards labeled for each of your students. To assign your daily jobs, place a different child's name card in each of the bear's pockets everyday.

Jenna Ott—Gr. 2, Mother Seton School, Emmitsburg, MD

Quick And Easy Attendance

Taking attendance has seasonal flair with this eye-catching chart. To make the chart, label a sheet of poster board with the title and directions as shown; then mount it on a bulletin board. Insert rows of pushpins (one pin for each student). Each month make a set of seasonal nametags for your students (Sept.—apples, Oct.—pumpkins, Nov.—turkeys, Dec.—Christmas trees, etc.). Punch a hole in the top of each nametag using a hole puncher. Suspend each nametag from a pushpin. When students enter the room each day, they remove their nametags and place them in a box in a designated location. At a glance you can see the names of students who are absent. Have a child return the nametags to the chart at the end of each day.

Carol Mack—Gr. 2, Casselberry Elementary School, Casselberry, FL

What's For Lunch?

This convenient chart allows you to record your lunch count quickly and easily. To make a chart, mount a library-book pocket for each student onto a sheet of poster board. Write a different student's name on each pocket. From colored tagboard, cut small strips to represent various lunch selections. For example, a blue strip = buying lunch, a red strip = brought lunch, a yellow strip = buying milk. (You may need to add different colored strips to represent other selections offered at your school.) Display the board in a prominent location. Store the strips in a basket near the lunch-count board. When students enter the room, they place the appropriately colored strips in their mounted pockets. This system also allows you to easily take attendance because absent students' pockets will be empty.

Alison Taylor—Gr. 4, Wexford Elementary, Wexford, PA

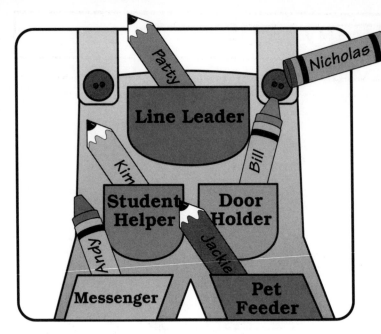

Overall Job Chart

Cut out a pair of overalls from a large piece of blue bulletin-board paper. From different colors of construction paper, cut several pockets. Label each pocket with a class job. Glue the edges of the pockets to the overalls, leaving the top of each pocket open. Make nametags by cutting crayon-shaped cutouts from colored construction paper. Label a cutout for each child. To use the chart, place a different child's crayon cutout in each pocket of the overalls. The child whose name is in each pocket performs the task written on that pocket. Rotate students' jobs at the end of each week.

Kristie Cobb, Sam Houston Elementary, Bryan, TX

Clip-On Lunch Count

Here's a convenient way to tell which students brought their lunches to school and which students are buying their lunches. Create a helpers chart from a sheet of poster board. Draw a line down the center of the poster board with a dark marker to make two columns. At the bottom of the first column, draw a picture of a lunch tray. At the bottom of the second column, draw a picture of a lunchbox. Mount this chart in a prominent location. Next, label a clothespin for each child. When students enter the room each day, they clip their clothespins in the appropriate columns.

Kim Ennis—Gr. K, Smith's Station Primary School, Smiths, AL

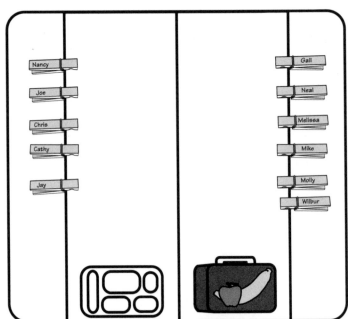

Duty Wheel

Easily rotate students' classroom duties with this display. To make a duty wheel, cut out a large tagboard circle. Divide the circle into the desired number of sections as shown. Label each section with a classroom duty. Mount the duty wheel to your bulletin board. Next, label a craft-size clothespin for each child. Clip the clothespins to sections of the duty wheel to indicate students' jobs for the week. At the end of each week, rotate the clothespins clockwise to assign new duties. (Depending on the number of students in your class and the number of duties on your duty wheel, it may be necessary to rotate certain students out each week.)

Nancy Walker—Gr. 4, Fall Creek Elementary School, Fall Creek, WI

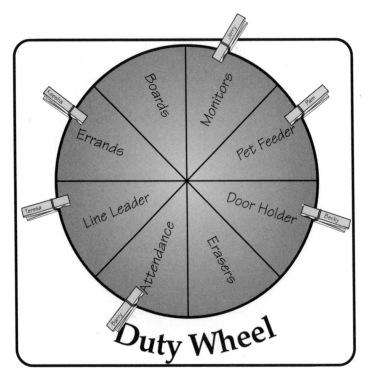

Create beautiful bulletin-board backgrounds by using plastic tablecloths. These tablecloths are available in a variety of colors and patterns that will brighten all of your displays. And they can be used from year to year because they won't fade!

Ginny Schram—Gr. 2, Liverpool Elementary, Liverpool, NY

This dynamite door decoration is simply out of this world! Cover your door with black bulletin-board paper. Mount a sun cutout, an earth cutout, and several planet cutouts (labeled for each subject) near the top of the door. Then mount a rocket cutout and the title to the door as shown. Attach strips of red and yellow curling ribbon to the base of the rocket for flames. Complete the display by attaching star cutouts (with students' photographs and names in the centers) along the door frame.

Ashley Head—Substitute teacher, Thorsby, AL

This display holds a special surprise for each of your students. Mount a large mailbox cutout in the center of your board. Around the mailbox attach a small, labeled envelope for each child. Place a personalized letter inside each child's envelope to be read on the first day of school.

At a later date, modify your display. Duplicate the stamp pattern on page 23 for each child. Have students design stamps to represent their personalities. Then remove the envelopes from your display and mount the decorative stamps.

Julie Eick Granchelli, Warren P. Towne Elementary School, Medina, NY

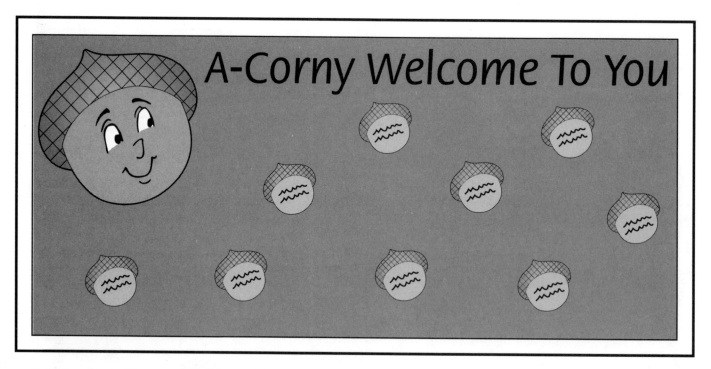

First-day jitters disappear with this combination display and activity. Mount the title and the large acorn character on your bulletin board. Then cut out a small acorn from colored construction paper for each child in your class. Write a corny joke on the front of each acorn and the punch line on the back; then mount the acorns on your board. In turn, have each student choose an acorn and read the joke. Allow time for students to answer; then have the child read the punch line. When the class stops giggling, ask the child to tell a bit about himself.

Dawn M. Pierson—Gr. 3, Ridge Meadows School, Ellisville, MO

You Fit Right In!

Students assemble personalized puzzle pieces to create this fantastic bulletin board. Cut a large square of paper into puzzle pieces for your students. Label each piece with a different child's name. As students enter your classroom on the first day of school, give each one his own puzzle piece and have him color it. When the children have colored their pieces, work together to assemble them on your bulletin board. Ask students with edge pieces to approach the board first to form the puzzle's border; then allow the remaining students to determine the position of their pieces. Pin the pieces to the board as they fit in place. This activity not only makes an attractive display, but also helps students work cooperatively.

Therese Durhman—Gr. 5, Mountain View School, Hickory, NC

This attractive bulletin board encourages critical thinking skills. Using an opaque projector, enlarge the patterns on pages 25 and 26 to the desired sizes. Cut out and color each pattern and attach it to the bulletin board as shown. Add dimension to the display with the following techniques.

— To make hair for the child, glue strands of yarn to a paper circle the same size as the child's head as shown on page 26. When the glue is dry, gather the strands on each side of the child's head with bows to make pigtails.

— To make shingles on the roof of the well, overlap squares of brown construction paper and attach them with a stapler.

Jenny Zollers—Gr. 1, Kenilworth Elementary School, Bowie, MD

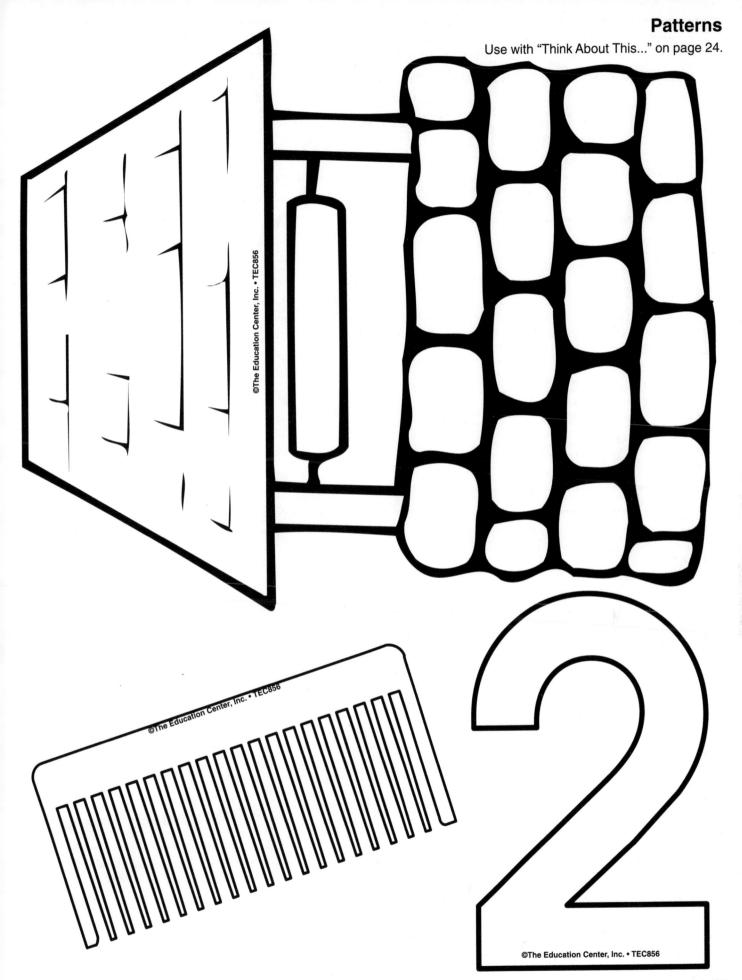

©The Education Center, Inc. • TEC856

©The Education Center, Inc. • TEC856

©The Education Center, Inc. • TEC856

Patterns

Use with "Think About This" on page 24.

©The Education Center, Inc. • TEC856

26

This personalized autumn display is sure to brighten your room. Mount the title and the tree-trunk cutout on your bulletin board. Using orange, brown, yellow, and red construction paper, cut out a fall leaf for each of your students and attach each child's photograph to a leaf. Staple the leaves on and around the tree cutout to complete your display.

Tamala S. Geiger—Grs. K –1, St. James School, Trenton, NJ

This bulletin board describes your students. Mount the title on your board. Duplicate the frame pattern on page 28 for each child. Have each child color a self-portrait inside the frame. Then have the child write her name and several descriptive words about herself at the bottom of the frame. Mount the completed projects on your board.

Stella Levy—Gr. 3, Hackley School, Tarrytown, NY

Pattern

Use with "Now Introducing…" on page 27.

This student-made display brightens any bulletin board. Provide your students with yellow construction paper, scissors, glue, markers, and other desired materials. Ask each child to design and make her own unique sun. Mount the completed projects on a background of blue bulletin-board paper and add your title.

Karen Saner—Grs. K-1, Burns Elementary, Burns, KS

Personalize your bulletin board with the help of your students. Duplicate the child pattern on page 30 for each of your students. Have each child cut out his pattern and then write his name in the space on the book bag. Then have the child color his pattern to resemble himself. Mount students' completed pictures along with the title for a cheerful display.

Carol Hocevar—Gr. 5, St. Bridget School, Parma, OH

Pattern

Use with "Look Who's In Our Class!" on page 29.

Name

Portray your children as the "fairest of them all" with this charming display. Mount the title on your bulletin board. Then trace the mirror pattern on page 32 on black construction paper for each child. Cut out the mirror shapes and glue an oval of foil in the center of each mirror. Staple the mirrors to your bulletin board. During the first week of school, have each child color a picture of her face on a five-inch circle of white construction paper. Attach each child's illustration to the center of a mirror to complete your display.

Jodi Cohen—Gr. 3, Kimball Hill School, Rolling Meadows, IL

Attract students' interest with this fall display. Mount the Rollerblade character and the title on your bulletin board. Then have each child design, cut out, and decorate a construction-paper Rollerblade. Have students use yarn for laces and plastic milk-jug caps for wheels. On his cutout, have each child write his name and his academic goal for the year. Staple the Rollerblades around the character to complete the display.

Nancy M. Grow—Gr. 5, Westchester School, Kirkwood, MO

Pattern

Use with "Mirror, Mirror, On The Wall" on page 31.

Your students are in bloom with this attractive display. Photograph each of your students on the first day of school. After developing the film, glue each photo to the center of a flower cutout. Mount the flowers with stems and leaves on a garden bulletin board.

Pam Boullé—Gr. K, Jupiter Elementary, Palm Bay, FL

This display holds a bus-load of smiles. Mount a large bus cutout on a board. Have children color and cut out illustrations of themselves to be mounted in or on the bus. You're sure to hear compliments on this attractive display.

Jayne M. Gammons—Gr. K, Oak Grove Elementary, Durham, NC

Shining Stars

Take a Polaroid snapshot of each of your children on the first day of school. While waiting for the pictures to develop, discuss the idea that each child possesses unique and special qualities. Using the pattern on page 35, have each child trace a star on yellow construction paper or tagboard and cut it out. Then have each child glue his photograph to the center of the star. Have the child use a brightly colored marker to write words and sentences describing his special qualities around the photograph. Invite students to share their qualities with one another. Then display all of the stars on your bulletin board.

Deborah Abrams—Gr. 5, Laguna Elementary, Laguna, NM

Back-To-School Quilt

A rtistic N ice N eat	G iving I ntelligent N ice A dorable	E xcellent L ovable E njoyable N ice	J ovial E njoyable R eal O utstanding D arling	B londe R adical A wesome D ear	J aunty E xcellent N ice
D ear A ttractive W onderful N eat	B rave O ldest B oy	T errific I maginative M arvelous	T errific O ver 6 years M odest	T op-notch R eal I ntelligent S ensitive H appy	A wesome R adical T errific
T op-notch O ldest D ear D ancer	C lever A lert T errific H elpful Y oung	B eautiful E xcellent C aring C ute A dorable	S hy A rtistic M odest	K een E xcellent V aluable I ntelligent N ice	L ovable U seful C ute Y oung

This display not only is attractive, but also makes students feel welcome in your class. Mount different colored construction-paper squares to your bulletin board. In each square, write a child's name vertically down the left side of the square. Then horizontally write a descriptive word that corresponds with each letter of the child's name.

Angie Kelley—Gr. 1, Weaver Elementary, Anniston, AL

©The Education Center, Inc. • TEC856

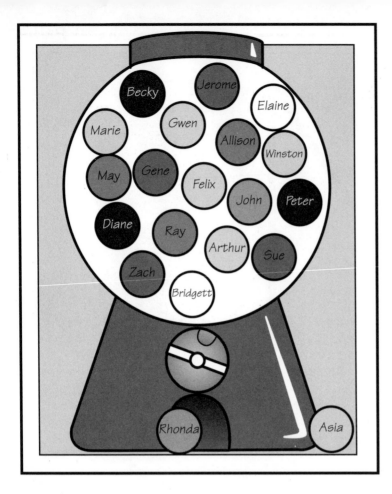

Welcome your new students with this cheerful door decoration. Using bulletin-board paper, design a large gumball-machine cutout. Mount the cutout on your door. Cut out a gumball shape from colored construction paper for each of your students. Label each gumball with a different child's name and attach it to the machine.

VaReane Gray Heese—Gr. 2, Omaha, NE

Get off to a clean start with this eye-catching display. Mount the title to your bulletin board. Then extend a length of string across your board for a clothesline. Cut out a construction-paper T-shirt for each of your students (see pattern on page 38). Label each shirt with a child's name and attach the shirts to the clothesline. Next attach a washing-machine cutout to the board. For a realistic look, place a small amount of soap and water in a resealable plastic bag and seal the bag tightly. Tape the bag behind the window of the washing machine. Make a laundry basket by cutting a plastic basket in half. Attach the basket to the board. Place a few items of clothing inside the basket to complete the display.

Cindy Sweeney—Gr. 3, Homan Elementary, Schererville, IN

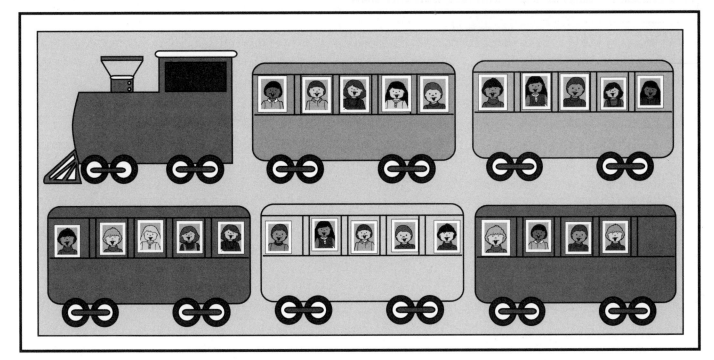

Showcase students' smiling faces year-round with a variety of photo displays. Photograph each of your students on the first day of school; then laminate the photographs. Create seasonal displays using the photos for cheerful accents. Suggestions for fall displays are listed below.

September—train or a school bus display with students' photographs in the windows.
October—students' photos displayed in pumpkin cutouts.
November—students' photos displayed in turkey cutouts.
December—each child's photo in the top of a Christmas stocking cutout.

Christy Owens—Gr. K, West Alexandria Elementary, West Alexandria, OH

Students contribute to this bulletin board to create a bright and cheerful display. On a blue sky background, mount the sun cutout and the title. Then attach two lengths of yarn or string across the board to make clotheslines. Duplicate the T-shirt pattern on page 38 on construction paper for each of your students. Cut out the T-shirts and label each one with a child's name. Then have students decorate their T-shirts using crayons and other desired materials. Staple the completed T-shirts to the clotheslines as shown.

Rona Forman—Gr. K, Mill Basin School, Brooklyn, NY

Pattern

Use with "Hanging Out In Third Grade Is Loads Of Fun" on page 36 and "Kindergarten Suits Us To A *'T'*" on page 37.

©The Education Center, Inc. • TEC856

Here's a bulletin-board display that helps inform parents of their children's school-supply needs. On your board, mount a large cutout of a bear holding a chart. Attach a different library book pocket to the chart for each item needed. On the outside of each pocket, write the name of an item or attach a picture of the item such as pencils, paper, crayons, or glue. Duplicate notes for each item (see the reproducible on page 40) and place them in the pockets. When a student needs an item, she selects the appropriate note from the display to take home to her parent.

Dianne Neumann—Gr. 2, Frank C. Whiteley School, Hoffman Estates, IL

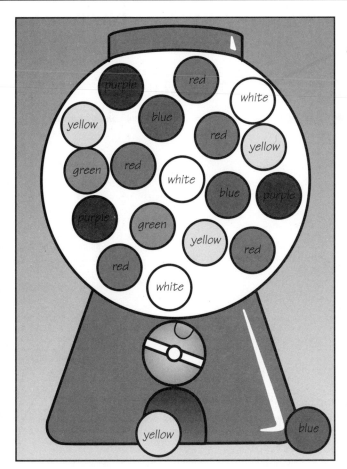

This display for young children can be adapted throughout the school year. Mount the bubble-gum machine cutout to your bulletin board. Then cut out construction-paper circles for gumballs. (See the suggestions below.) Attach pieces of Velcro to the bubble-gum machine. Then attach the opposite pieces of Velcro to the backs of the circles. Attach the gumballs to the machine. Encourage students to touch and manipulate the bubble-gum circles.

Bubble-gum suggestions:
— Cover the front of the circles with different textured materials such as sandpaper, cotton balls, foil, plastic packing pieces, and rug samples.
— Cut the circles from different colors of construction paper. Label the circles with the corresponding color words.
— Label the circles with letters of the alphabet.

Joanne Jostes—Pre-K, Christian Family Day Care, Hazelwood, MO

I need pencils

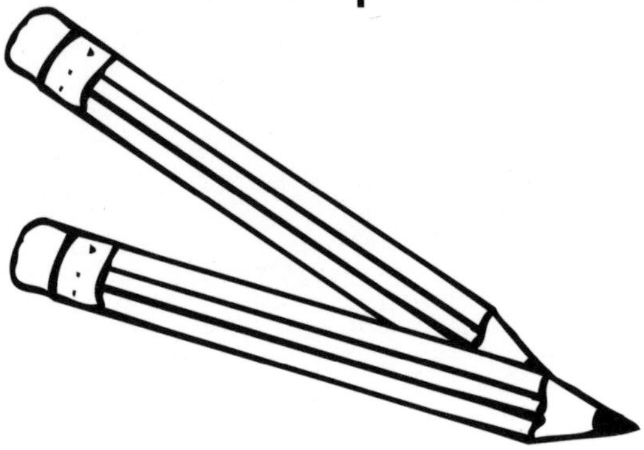

for school.

I need crayons

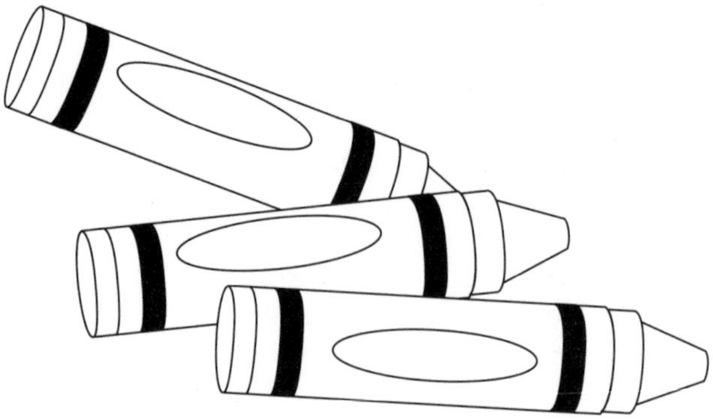

for school.

I need paper

for school.

I need glue

for school.

I need

_____

for school.

I need

_____

for school.

Note To Teacher: Use with "Be Cool—Be Ready For School!" on page 39.

BACK-TO-SCHOOL ACTIVITIES

Pop!

Start your school year off with a bang! Before school begins, prepare a getting-to-know-you question on a small piece of paper for each child in your class. Roll up each piece of paper tightly and place it inside a deflated balloon. Then blow up the balloons and attach one to each child's chair with a length of string. On the first day of school, have the children find their desks, pop their balloons, and read their questions. To complete the activity, gather all students together to share the answers to their questions.

Jeannette Freeman—Grade 3, Baldwin School of Puerto Rico, Guaynabo, PR

Letters From Last Year

At the end of your current school year, have each student write a letter to the child who will be occupying his seat next year. In the letter, have the child explain the class rules, rewards, and procedures. Also have the child list other important things the new student should know. At the beginning of the next school year, present the students with their letters. Students are sure to feel a bit less anxious after reading these informative messages.

Diana Boykin, DeZavala Elementary, Midland, TX

Let's Read About School!

Young children often feel anxious on the first day of school. Show your youngsters that their feelings are not unusual by reading literature about the first day of school (such as *Little Critter's This Is My School* by Mercer Mayer [Western Publishing Company, 1990]). In no time at all, your youngsters will feel at ease with the school experience.

Kathleen Darby—Gr. 1, Community School, Cumberland, RI

Personalized Folders

As each child enters your room on the first day of school, welcome him with his own folder. Inside the folder, place an interest inventory, a few fun sheets, and a personal welcome letter from you. This helps ease the first-day jitters and provides students with fun work to do at the beginning of the day.

Julie Eick Granchelli, Warren P. Towne Elementary School, Medina, NY

It's In The Bag!

This great guessing game is a perfect ice breaker for the first day of school. Label each of seven paper grocery bags with a different letter of the word *WELCOME*. In each bag, place several items that begin with the letter on the bag. For example, the *W* bag might have items such as a walnut, a wheel, and a wig. Display the bags in order for your students. Then ask your children to take turns guessing the items in each bag. (You may have students guess the items aloud or by writing their answers on paper.) If desired, award a small prize to the student who correctly guesses the most items in the bags.

Tracy Hughes—Gr. 2, Baker Elementary, Birmingham, AL

New-Student Bags

Be prepared for the arrival of new students after the beginning week of school. Fill a large, resealable plastic bag with items such as a nametag, informative parent notes, an activity calendar, and other items that your students received during the first week of school. When a new student joins your class, simply give him his bag of supplies, and he's all set!

Heidi L. Hoffman—Gr. 1, Pershing Elementary, Lincoln, NE

Opening-Day Cassette Tape

New students often join your class after the first day of school. To avoid reviewing all of your first-day information with each child, try this convenient tip. Simply make a tape recording of vital information that is shared, such as supplies needed, procedures, and schedules. When a new student joins your class, have her listen to the tape and take notes on the information.

Julie Eick Granchelli, Warren P. Towne Elementary School, Medina, NY

Beginning- And End-Of-The-Year Photos

Be sure to bring your camera to photograph each child at the beginning of the school year. Collect the pictures for safekeeping and as the end of the year approaches, take another photograph. Then present each child with both pictures on the last day of school to let her see how much she has grown.

Debbie Christophersen—Grs. 4–5, North Love Christian School, Rockford, IL

Kindergarten Welcome Bags

Help kindergartners feel welcome with fun special-meaning bags. For each child, fill a paper lunch bag with the following items: a cotton ball, a chocolate kiss, a sticker, a rubber band, a penny, a construction-paper star, a tissue, a toothpick, a bandage, a length of gold thread, an eraser, and a Life Saver candy. Duplicate and cut out the notes on page 43. Write a child's name on each note and place each note in a bag. Have the children find the items in their bags as you read the special note to them. Then have them take their bags home to share their welcome messages with their parents.

Michelle Therrien—Grs. K–2, Bright Horizons Children's Center, Pittsfield, MA

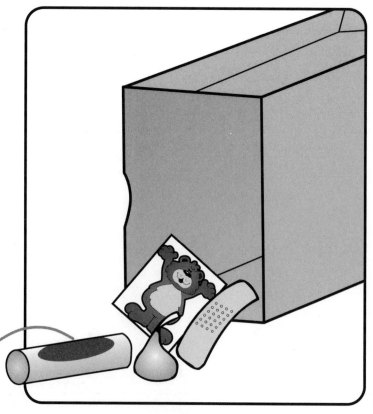

Welcome!

Dear _____,

  Welcome to your new classroom. The items in this bag have special meanings.

—The cotton ball is to remind you that this room is full of kind words and warm feelings.

—The chocolate kiss is to comfort you when you are feeling sad.

—The sticker is to remind you that we will all stick together and help each other.

—The rubber band is to remind you to hug someone.

—The penny is to remind you that you are valuable and special.

—The star is to remind you to shine and always try your best.

—The tissue is to remind you to help dry someone's tears.

—The toothpick is to remind you to "pick out" the good qualities in your classmates and in yourself.

—The bandage is to remind you to heal hurt feelings in your friends and in yourself.

—The gold thread is to remind you that friendship ties our hearts together.

—The eraser is to remind you that everyone makes mistakes and that it is okay.

—The Life Saver is to remind you that you can come to me if you need someone to talk to.

With love,

©The Education Center, Inc. • TEC856

Welcome!

Dear _____,

  Welcome to your new classroom. The items in this bag have special meanings.

—The cotton ball is to remind you that this room is full of kind words and warm feelings.

—The chocolate kiss is to comfort you when you are feeling sad.

—The sticker is to remind you that we will all stick together and help each other.

—The rubber band is to remind you to hug someone.

—The penny is to remind you that you are valuable and special.

—The star is to remind you to shine and always try your best.

—The tissue is to remind you to help dry someone's tears.

—The toothpick is to remind you to "pick out" the good qualities in your classmates and in yourself.

—The bandage is to remind you to heal hurt feelings in your friends and in yourself.

—The gold thread is to remind you that friendship ties our hearts together.

—The eraser is to remind you that everyone makes mistakes and that it is okay.

—The Life Saver is to remind you that you can come to me if you need someone to talk to.

With love,

©The Education Center, Inc. • TEC856

Note To Teacher: Duplicate copies of this page to use with "Kindergarten Welcome Bags" on page 42.

43

Paul Sneeringer
#5

School Leaders

Help students recognize leaders in their school by using the pattern of the book *Brown Bear, Brown Bear, What Do You See?* by Bill Martin, Jr. Obtain pictures of several leaders such as the school principal, the assistant principal, and the lunchroom manager. On a sheet of chart paper, write verses similar to the verses used in *Brown Bear, Brown Bear...* as shown. Attach school-leader photographs in the appropriate places. Your youngsters will enjoy chanting these personalized verses while learning to recognize important people in their school.

Marcia Boone and Robin Gattis—Gr. K, Seagoville Elementary School, Seagoville, TX

Bus Number Tags

Help students remember their bus numbers with personalized tags. Using the pattern on page 45, duplicate a bus tag on yellow construction paper for each of your bus riders. Write each child's name and bus number on her tag. Have bus students cut out and fold their tags when they arrive at school. Then have the students display their bus tags on their desks for several days until they have memorized their bus numbers.

Lenora Norris—Gr. 1, Suwanee School, Suwanee, GA

I see Ms. Bailey looking at me.

Review Jeopardy

Assess students' retention of the previous year's material with an exciting skills-review game. To set up the game, label several construction-paper squares with categories such as math, spelling, language arts, science, or social studies. Staple them along the top of your bulletin board. Label one side of each of several more squares with a question relating to a category and a point value on the other side. Pin the squares below the corresponding categories with the point values faceup. To play the game, divide your students into teams. In turn, have a child from each team choose a card by naming a category and a point value. Have one student—acting as the game-show host—read the question on the card for the child to answer. If the child answers correctly, she earns points for her team. If her answer is incorrect, the question may be answered by another team. If no correct answer is given, another square is chosen. Play continues until all of the questions have been answered. The team with the greatest number of points wins.

Andrea Johnson—Grs. 1–3, Blanton Elementary, St. Petersburg, FL

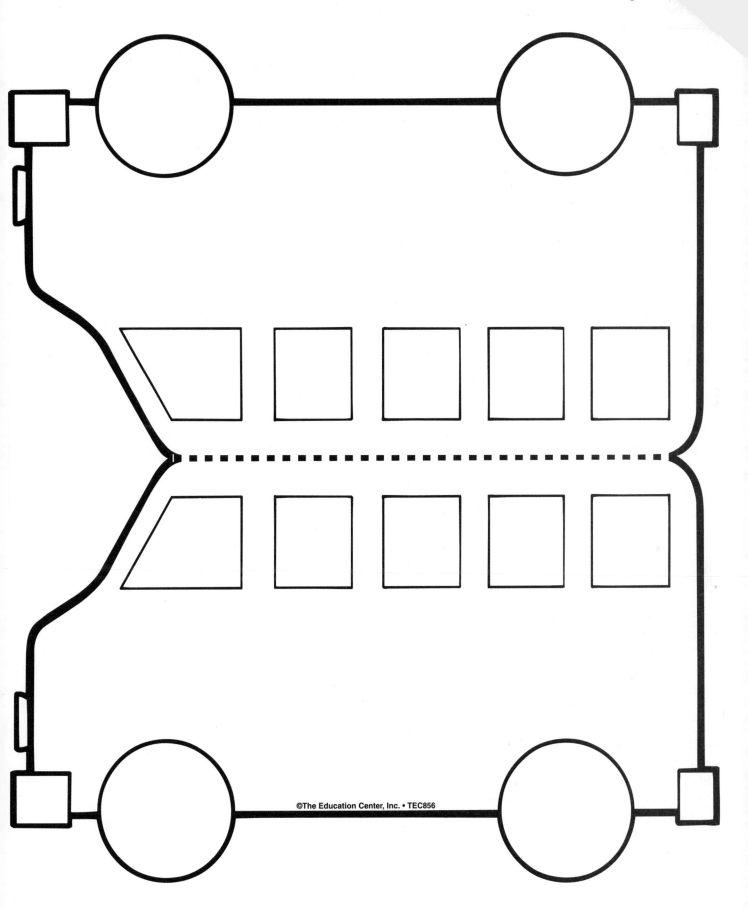

©The Education Center, Inc. • TEC856

People Puzzle

Pattern
on page 44.

...ether on the first day of school helps stu-
... team. On one side of a large sheet of
... a brightly colored picture with a fun class
... On the opposite side, divide the tagboard
... eces (one piece for each child) using a
marker. Then cut the pieces apart on the lines. As each student enters your room on the first day of school, give her a
puzzle piece. Have each child write her name and color a
design on the plain side of the piece. When all students
have completed this step, have students take turns showing
their puzzle pieces and introducing themselves. Then have
students gather together on the floor to assemble the class
puzzle. Students turn their pieces over to the picture sides
and work together to reveal the picture.

Cynthia S. McKinney, Centerville, OH

Personal Time Capsule

This activity helps students compare their preferences at
the beginning and the ending of school. Duplicate the reproducible on page 47; then program numbers 12, 13, and
14 with additional questions. Duplicate the page for each
of your students. Have each child complete the page, writing her responses in the right-hand column. Then have the
child fold her paper backwards on the dotted line as shown.
Collect students' papers and store them until the end of the
year. During the last week of school, have each child complete the page once again, writing her responses in the left-
hand column. When students have completed their pages,
have them unfold their papers and compare their current
responses to those given at the beginning of the year.

Linda Harris—Gr. 2, Dobbs Elementary, Rockwall, TX

School Map

Your older students will enjoy this mapping activity. On
the first day of class, take students on a tour of the school.
Encourage students to note the locations of the classrooms
and offices. Upon returning to your classroom, draw a map
of the school on your chalkboard with the help of your students' verbal instructions. If desired, have each child copy
the map on a piece of paper for future reference.

*Julie Eick Granchelli, Warren P. Towne Elementary School,
Medina, NY*

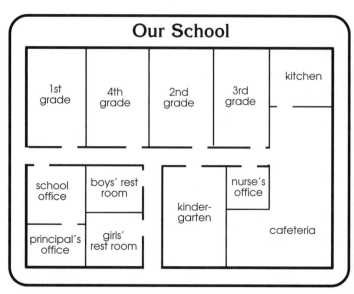

Name _____

A Time Capsule About Me

	May	September
1. date		
2. full name		
3. favorite color		
4. best friend		
5. favorite game		
6. favorite T.V. show		
7. favorite book		
8. favorite sport		
9. favorite song		
10. favorite food		
11. what I want to be when I grow up		
12. _____		
13. _____		
14. _____		

Note To Teacher: Use with "Personal Time Capsule" on page 46.

47

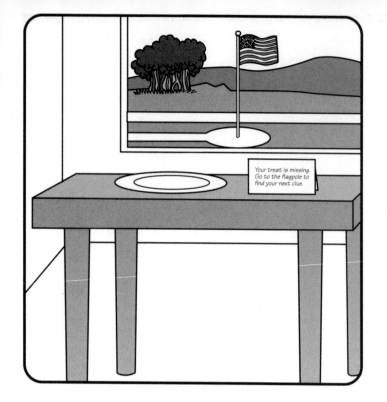

Treasure Hunt

This exciting activity helps young children learn their way around school and meet some important people. To begin the activity, set out a plate of snacks and tell children that they will be eating the snacks after a short recess outside. Arrange to have a colleague hide the snacks while the class is outside, leaving only a note in place of the snacks. When students return to the classroom, read the note which contains a clue such as, "Your treat is missing. Go to the flagpole to find your next clue." Take your class to the flagpole and read the next clue which might say, "Go to the lunchroom to find your next clue." In the lunchroom, introduce the children to the cafeteria workers and show students where they will sit for lunch. Continue the treasure hunt, taking your children to places such as the library, the office, and the bathrooms. Finally, have the last clue lead your students back to your classroom to find the snacks hidden in your room.

Gloria Bartoloni and Michelle Prentice-Smith—Gr. K, Mabel Paine School, Yorba Linda, CA

Predicting Activities To Come

Involve your students in a predicting activity during the first week of school. List on the board several of the topics, projects, and units in which your students will participate during the year. Then have students write several paragraphs telling which activities they think they will most enjoy and why they think they will enjoy them. Save the papers until the end of the year. During the last month of school, have each student write another paper telling which activities he most enjoyed during the year. Distribute the papers written at the beginning of the year and have students compare their prediction papers to their final papers.

Myra Cohen—Gr. 6, HANC School, Plainview, NY

Chocolate Kiss Notes

End your first day of school with notes of sweetness. Duplicate the note on page 49 for each child in your class. Attach chocolate kisses to the tops of the notes and present them to your students. Students are sure to enjoy these tasty treats.

Lessie Boudreaux—Gr. 3, Temple Elementary, Diboll, TX

Attach chocolate kiss here.

Thank you for making our first day terrific! You deserve a kiss!

See you tomorrow.

©The Education Center, Inc. • TEC856

Attach chocolate kiss here.

Thank you for making our first day terrific! You deserve a kiss!

See you tomorrow.

©The Education Center, Inc. • TEC856

Polaroid Alphabet

Create an eye-catching alphabet border of your students' smiling faces. Take one Polaroid snapshot of all students whose names begin with the letter *A*. Label that photo with a capital and a lowercase *a*. Below the letters, write the names of the children in the photo. Attach the photo below the *A* in your alphabet line. Group students alphabetically, take a picture for each letter represented, and attach each photo below the appropriate letter.

Leslie Lee—Gr. K, Deerwood Elementary, Poinciana, FL

Aa:
Alison, Angie, Abel

Hot-Potato Name Game

Generate excitement with this fast-moving game. Duplicate a potato nametag from page 51 on brown construction paper for each child. Cut out and label a tag for each child and attach it to her clothing. Have your students sit on the floor in a circle. Begin the game by having the children pass a potato, a beanbag, or a small ball as music plays. When the music stops, the child holding the "potato" says her own name and the name of a classmate. Continue in this manner, allowing all students to participate.

Tamala S. Geiger—Grs. K–1, St. James School, Trenton, NJ

Spell That Name

Challenge your students with this multi-faceted name game. For each child, prepare a 12" x 4" strip of construction paper labeled with her name. Write each child's name on another strip of paper and cut the letters apart. Place the letters from each child's name in an envelope. To begin the activity, have each child hold up her name strip as she introduces herself; then attach the strip to your chalkboard or bulletin board. Distribute an envelope of letter cards to each, making sure that no child receives her own set of letters. Have each child sequence the letters in her envelope to form one of her classmates' names. Encourage the children to use the name strips for references. When each student has successfully sequenced his letter cards, have him match the name to the correct student by taking the name strip from the bulletin board and returning it to its owner.

Tina Brown—Special Education Grs. 5–6, Van Cortlandtville Elementary School, Mohegan Lake, NY

Name Bingo

This game helps young children identify the letters in their names. Print each child's name on a piece of 12" x 4" tagboard or construction paper. Give each child his name strip and a supply of small construction-paper squares to use as markers. To play, call out a letter of the alphabet. Each child who has that letter in his name covers the letter on his name strip with a marker. The first student to cover all of the letters in his name is the winner. Reward the winner by having him call out the letters for the next game.

Rena Ezzell, St. Francis Xavier School, Ft. Myers, FL

Jack Be Nimble, Jack Be Quick

This nursery-rhyme activity helps students learn their classmates' names. After reciting the rhyme "Jack Be Nimble, Jack Be Quick" several times with your students, have your children act out the rhyme. Place an unlighted candle in a candle holder on the floor. Choose a child to jump over the candlestick as the class recites the rhyme, replacing the name *Jack* with that child's name. Continue in this manner until all students have had the chance to participate.

> Example:
> Brett be nimble,
> Brett be quick,
> Brett jump over the candlestick.

Kim Ennis—Gr. K, Smith's Station Primary School, Smiths, AL

Making Nametags

Keep students busy with making nametags as they enter the classroom. At a special supply table, provide squares of colored construction paper, pinking shears, crayons or markers, sequins, ribbon, yarn, glue, and pins or tape. Allow students to choose the materials of their choice to create imaginative nametags. Encourage students to be as creative as they please. When all students have arrived, have each child introduce himself and share his nametag creation with his classmates.

Sonya Franklin—Gr. 5, Pell City-Kennedy Elementary, Pell City, AL

Name In A Cup

Young children really benefit from this name-recognition activity. Give each child a cup with her name printed on the outside. Cut a supply of one-inch squares from construction paper. Label one square for each letter of the child's name; then place the squares inside the cup. Using the printed name on the cup as a reference, have the child sequence her letter squares to spell her name. At a later date, make the activity more challenging by covering the name on the cup with masking tape before the child sequences her letters.

Kim Yen Vu—Pre-K, Central Elementary, Palacios, TX

Bingo Board Game

Learning names is lots of fun with this game. Duplicate the gameboard on page 54 for each of your students. On each page, write your name in the center square; then write the name of a different child in each remaining square. Use a variety of name combinations on the gameboards. Give a gameboard and a supply of construction-paper game markers to each child. Allow the child to cover your name in the center square for a free space. To play the game, call out a child's name. Students whose gameboards contain that name cover the name with a marker. Continue calling out students' names. The first child to cover three names in a row is the winner.

Elaine Kaplan—Grs. 1–2, Link Elementary School, New City, NY

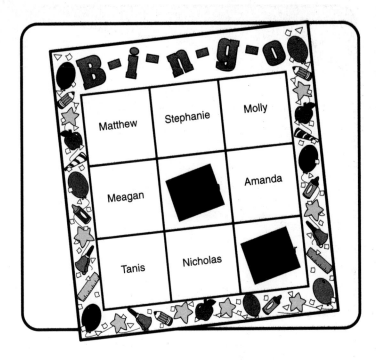

Thematic Nametags

This thematic nametag system helps group your students for field trips. Choose a classroom nametag theme at the beginning of the year such as animals, flowers, or toys. Using a die-cut machine or a tracer, cut the desired shapes from construction paper. For example, if a flower theme is used for a group of 30 students, cut six tags each from yellow, green, pink, red, and blue construction paper. Write each child's name on a shape and have the child decorate her shape as desired. Laminate the nametags; then punch a hole in each tag using a hole puncher. Tie a loop of yarn through the hole for suspending the nametag around the child's neck. Using a permanent marker, write the school's name and phone number on the back of each tag.

Pam Boullé—Gr. K, Jupiter Elementary, Palm Bay, FL

Who's Missing?

This mystery game helps students learn the names of their classmates. To play, have all students cover their eyes. Secretly choose one child to step outside of the room. Then have the remaining students open their eyes and try to guess who is missing from the room. When the missing child is identified, have her return to the room. Continue play in this manner until all of your students have had the opportunity to be the missing child. For added fun, select two or three children at a time to leave the room.

Marcia Boone and Robin Gattis—Gr. K, Seagoville Elementary School, Seagoville, TX

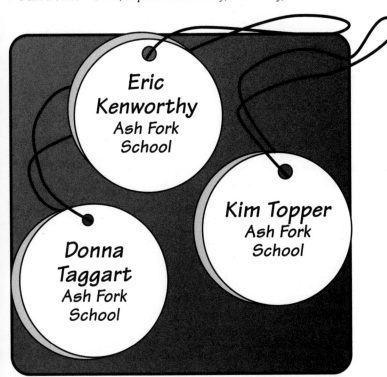

Butter-Lid Nametags

Save plastic lids from empty butter containers to make durable nametags. To make a nametag, use a hole puncher to punch a hole in the lid. Then tie a two-foot loop of yarn through the hole. Write the child's first and last names and your school name on the lid using a permanent marker. Have students wear these nametags for field trips and when you have substitute teachers or guest speakers.

VaReane Gray Heese—Gr. 2, Omaha, NE

BINGO

Note To Teacher: Use the page with "Bingo Board Game" on page 53.

GETTING ACQUAINTED

Poetic Introductions

Using the dictionary and the thesaurus is lots of fun with this activity. Have each child write her name in capital letters vertically on the left side of her paper. Then, using a dictionary and a thesaurus, have the child look for self-descriptive words or phrases beginning with the letters of her name. Have her write the words or phrases next to the appropriate letters as shown. After revising and editing their name poems, have students glue their poems to creatively designed construction-paper backgrounds for display.

Stella Levy—Gr. 3, Hackley School, Tarrytown, NY

Partner Portraits

Students color their way into new friendships with this creative project. Divide your students into pairs. Have students in each pair face one another and draw pictures of each other. Encourage students to color their partners using the proper hair color and clothing patterns. When the pictures are completed, have students ask their partners questions about their families, their friends, and their likes and dislikes. Below each child's picture, have him write a few sentences describing his partner. Display these colorful creations to add instant appeal to your classroom.

Jacqueline Halpern—Gr. 2, Great Neck, NY

Jumping for joy to be in the third grade.

Involved in Girl Scouts.

Loves pizza.

Lives in New York.

Pairing Up Friends

This mingling activity encourages young children to use visual-descrimination and matching skills. Prepare for the activity by obtaining several different patterns of wallpaper. From each pattern of wallpaper, cut two pencil shapes using the pattern on page 56. On the first day of school, give each child a pencil shape. Have the students mingle with one another to find the students with the matching patterns. When students find their partners, have them sit down together and visit with one another.

adapted from an idea by Peggy Sloan—Gr. Pre-K, Oak Forest Park District, Oak Forest, IL

Patterns
Use with "Pairing Up Friends" on page 55.

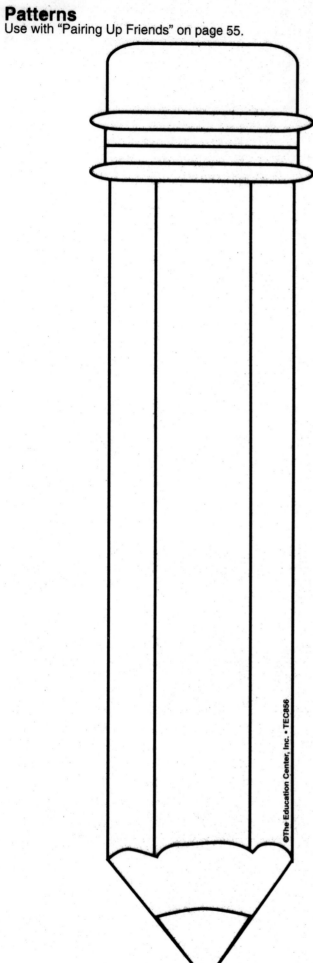

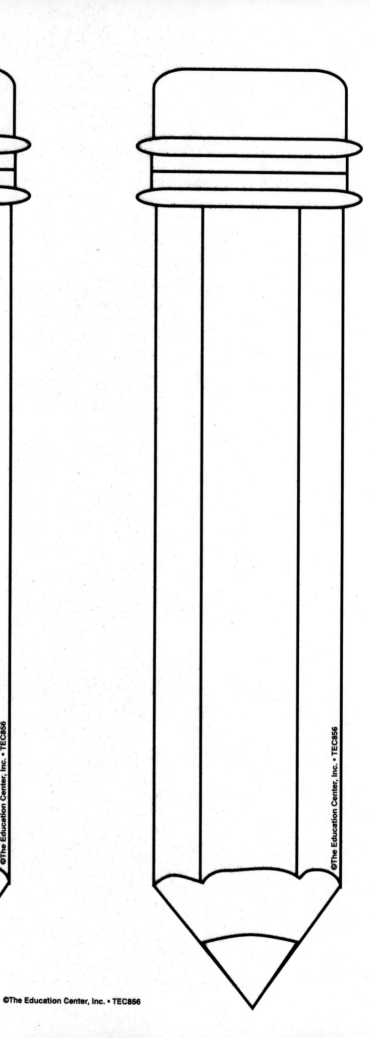

©The Education Center, Inc. • TEC856

©The Education Center, Inc. • TEC856

©The Education Center, Inc. • TEC856

Interview Desktags

This fun partner activity gives students the opportunity to make personalized desktags for one another. Divide your students into pairs. Have each student interview his partner, asking questions about his partner's family, hobbies, likes, and dislikes. When the interviews are complete, give each child a die-cut construction-paper tag or a sheet of paper from a fun-shaped notepad. Have each child write his partner's name in the center of the tag using a marker. Then, around the name, have the child write words or phrases to reveal the information gathered in the interview. Have each child present the tag to his partner. Then have the students attach the tags to their desks.

Jeannia Cribbs—Gr. 4, Foster Village Elementary, North Richland Hills, TX

Student Reporters

Here's a chance for your students to use their reporting skills. Duplicate the interview sheet on page 58 for each of your students. Divide your students into pairs. In turn, have students interview their partners using the questions on their sheets. Encourage students to ask some of their own questions and write the answers on the backs of their sheets. Complete the activity by having each student introduce his partner to the class and share a few interesting bits of information about him.

Lori Brandman—Gr. 5, Shallowford Falls Elementary, Marietta, GA

It's Time To Roll!

Roll out the fun with this get-acquainted activity. Pass around a roll of bathroom tissue to your students. Have each child tear off between one and five squares of tissue. Then, in turn, have each child share one piece of information about himself for each square of tissue that he took.

Debbie Grecco—Gr. 3, Northwest School, Butler, PA

Tasty Introductions

This yummy activity helps students get acquainted. Seat your students in a circle. Pass a bag of M&M's around the circle. Have each child take at least one M&M, but not more than five. In turn, have each child share one thing about herself for every M&M in her hand. When the child finishes sharing, she can eat her treat.

Michelle Therrien—Grs. Pre-K–1, Bright Horizons Children's Center, Pittsfield, MA

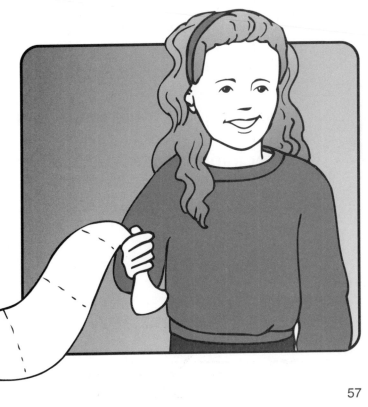

Attention All Reporters!

It's time for your first assignment. Interview one of your classmates and write the information in the spaces below.

Name: _____

Nickname: _____

Address: _____

Where were you born? _____

Have you ever lived in another state? _____

    If so, where? _____

What is your favorite T.V. show? _____

What is your favorite hobby? _____

Who is your favorite singer? _____

What is your favorite restaurant? _____

Other information: _____

_____

Reporter's signature:

_____

Note To Teacher: Use with "Student Reporters" on page 57.

Matching A Face To A [Name]

Young students enjoy this getting-to-kno[w]
Photograph each child on the first day of sc[hool]
double prints of your film. Mount one set of photographs
on poster board. Mount the remaining set of photos on
squares of poster board as shown to make photo cards.
Laminate the poster board and the photo cards for durability. Place the sheet of poster board on the floor. Have students place the photo cards atop the matching photos on
the board.

*Joanne Jostes—Gr. Pre-K, Christian Family Day Care,
Hazelwood, MO*

Who Am I?

This guessing game is a fun way for students to get acquainted. For each child, fold a small square of construction paper in half. On the outside of each folded square
write *Who Am I?* Then have each child write four clues
about himself inside his card. Collect each child's card before beginning the game. To play, choose one card and read
the clues inside. Allow students to make guesses after each
clue. Continue play in this manner until all students' cards
are read.

*Christine Fischer—Special Education Grs. 4-6, George J. Peters
School, Cranston, RI*

I have brown hair.
I am a girl.
I hate to wear dresses.
I have an older brother.

"Me Stew"

Look what's cooking in this getting-to-know-you activity. On the first day of school, display a large cooking pot
at the front of your room. If desired, decorate the outside of
the pot with the title ("Me Stew") and clip art of children.
Fill the pot with several items that describe you, your personality, your hobbies, and your family. When the school
day begins, introduce yourself to your students by remov-
ing one item at a time from the pot, explaining each item to
your class. Assign a day for each student to fill the Me-
Stew pot. Duplicate the parent letter on page 60 for each
child to take home. This letter encourages parents to help
their children choose the items to share with their classmates. Follow up this activity by reading the poem "Me-
Stew" in Shel Silverstein's *Where The Sidewalk Ends*.

Jody Tuskowski—Gr. 2, Madison Elementary, Stevens Point, WI

Dear Parent,

Your child will be participating in a getting-to-know-you activity entitled "Me Stew." Your child will need to bring to school three to five small items that describe his/her personality, hobbies, or interests. Items for this activity might include photographs, momentos, or small toys. Please assist your child in selecting interesting ingredients for his/her "Me Stew."

Sincerely,

_____

Please send these items to school by _____.

These items will be returned to you after being displayed in our classroom.

Me Stew

Getting To Know You

Each child plays a starring role with this sharing activity. Using a die-cut machine (or a simple pattern), cut out a supply of star shapes from yellow construction paper. Label each star with a question. (Sample questions are listed below.) Label a few of the stars with questions and the words *Wild Card*. Begin by placing the stars facedown on the floor. Have students gather around the stars in a circle. In turn, have each student choose a star and answer the question. If a child chooses a star labeled *Wild Card*, he answers the question and then asks you to answer the same question.

Sample questions:
What is your favorite board game to play?
What is your favorite outside game?
What is your favorite television show?
What is your favorite thing to do on a rainy day?
What is your favorite thing to do on weekends?
What is your favorite book?
If you could take any pet home from the zoo, what would it be?
If you could have three wishes, what would they be?
What would you do if you were the principal for a day?
Where would you love to go on vacation?

Dianne Neumann—Gr. 2, Frank C. Whiteley School, Hoffman Estates, IL

That's Me!

Before the beginning of school, contact each child's parent to obtain bits of information about the child such as favorite foods, family pets, and names of siblings. During the first few days of school, use spare moments to read the information about one of your students to the class. When the child recognizes that the information is about himself, he stands up and says, "That's me!"

Tina Brown—Special Education Grs. 5–6, Van Cortlandtville Elementary School, Mohegan Lake, NY

Question Of The Day

Get acquainted with your students with a roll-call game. Before taking attendance, ask a question such as "What is your favorite kind of animal?" When each child's name is called, she stands and answers the question. Ask a new question each day for the first few weeks of school.

Julie Eick Granchelli, Warren P. Towne Elementary School, Medina, NY

Class Dictionary

students review dictionary skills as they get to
one another with this class activity. As a class, review several dictionary entries. On a piece of paper, have
each child write her last name and her first name separated
by a comma. In parentheses, have the child write her name
using the pronunciation key. Then have the child write descriptions of her appearance, her personality, and her hobbies. After students revise and edit their descriptions, com-
pile the pages into a class dictionary and encourage students to read each others' entries. This dictionary is great
to display during Open House or parent/teacher confer-
ences.

*Lori Brandman—Gr. 5, Shallowford Falls Elementary,
Marietta, GA*

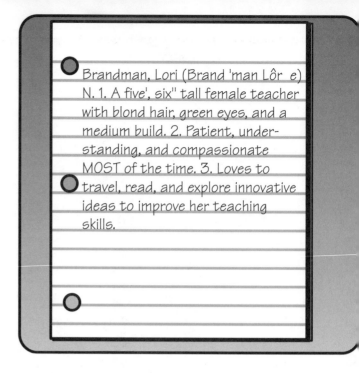

Survival Kit

Encourage students to get acquainted with this motivating activity. Have each child imagine that he is stranded
alone on an island for one week. Explain that food, water,
and shelter are provided. Then give each child a paper bag.
The child's assignment is to take the bag home and fill it
with four items that he would want to have with him on the
island. (If an item is too large for the bag, the child can
bring a picture or a drawing of the item.) The next day,
have each child share the items in his bag and tell why they
are important to him.

Diana Boykin, Midland, TX

Let's Get To Know Each Other

Students find this homework assignment truly entertaining. Write a letter to your class describing your family,
your interests, and other interesting information. Duplicate
the letter for each of your students. To do the assignment,
each student takes the letter home to read. Encourage each
child to share the letter with his parents as well. Then have
each child write a similar letter to you describing himself.

Lori Brandman, Marietta, GA

What's In The Bag?

Learn more about your students with this fun homework
project. On the first day of school, give each child a paper
lunch bag to take home. Have each child fill the bag with
five items from home that describe herself. The next day,
have the child tell about the items in her bag. Extend the
activity by creating individual books. To make a book
cover, duplicate the pattern on page 63 onto brown construction paper. Cut out the outline and laminate the cover,
if desired; then fold the cover in half on the dotted line. (If
desired, cut along the top of the cover with pinking shears
to give the cover a paper-bag look.) Label the cover as
shown. Duplicate and cut apart copies of page 64 for the
pages of the book. Stack several pages and staple them inside the cover. Have each child write or dictate information
about herself inside the book.

Terri B. Monroe—Gr. 1, St. Simon School, Indianapolis, IN

A

Paper Bag

Story

by

_____

Pattern

Note To Teacher: Use with "What's In The Bag?" on page 62.

We Are Family

This giant mobile helps students share with one another about their families. Prepare the main part of the mobile prior to this activity. To make the mobile, you need one hula hoop, one sturdy wooden hanger, and five yards of thin—but strong—rope. Cut the rope into four equal lengths. Tie one end of each length of rope to the hanger; then tie the opposite end of each length to the hula hoop as shown. Suspend the mobile using the hook of the wooden hanger.

During the first week of school, have students construct minimobiles about their families. Give each child a wire hanger, paper, crayons, and scissors. Have each child draw a small picture of each of his family members. Then have the child cut out each picture. Tape a length of string to each picture and have the child tie the strings to his hanger. In turn, have students share their mobiles with their classmates, introducing the members of their families. When all students have shared their projects, complete the giant mobile by suspending each minimobile from the hula hoop.

Fanny Páez, Cynthia Youens Elementary School, Houston, TX

Curious Critters

Here's a great way for students to share information about their home lives. Introduce a stuffed critter to your children such as a bear or a story character. Each day send the critter home with a different student. Then have each child write a letter to the class from the critter's point of view, describing what it saw at the child's home. Allow students to share their letters with their classmates.

Jo Bressan—Gr. 2, Jefferson Park School, El Paso, IL

ROUTINES

Tickets To Success

Encourage your students to work cooperatively toward positive behavior and work habits with this motivating system. Using the pattern on page 67, duplicate and cut apart a large supply of reward tickets on colored construction paper. Laminate the tickets for durability, if desired. Arrange your students' desks in groups of four to six. The students in each group work together to earn tickets by walking quietly in line, helping others, turning in homework, etc. You may also want to award tickets for test grades. Have each group store its tickets in a can or a box. At the end of each week, total the tickets and reward the winning group with a treat, free time, or a free homework day.

Coletta Preacely Ellis—Grs. 5–6, Wilson Elementary School, Lynwood, CA

Penny Power

This motivating behavior program also helps children practice money skills. In your class store, display four buckets labeled with different prices such as 3¢, 5¢, 8¢, and 10¢. Place small toys and treats of differing values in the buckets. Duplicate several copies of the penny sheet on page 68 and cut the pennies apart. Throughout the day, award students' positive behavior and work habits with these paper pennies. On designated days, allow students to buy items with their pennies. Students may choose to save their pennies to buy items of greater values. What a great incentive for good behavior!

Rhonda Souther—Gr. 1, Westwood Elementary School, Dalton, GA

Take Turns

Help young children practice taking turns with their classmates with a helpful buddy. Bring a doll or a stuffed animal to class and name it Take Turn. Use this doll to help with attendance each day by giving Take Turn to a student who says his own name and then passes the doll to a classmate. Have students continue in this manner until all students have had a turn. Take Turn is a helpful assistant during sharing time as well. Simply pass the doll to a student who then shares a story or an event with the class and then passes the doll to another child when he is finished .

Cheryl Van Arsdale—Grs. Preschool and Pre-K, Learning Steps Children's School, New Egypt, NJ

Name Cards

To make sure that all students are equally chosen to answer questions or to be helpers during the day, try this handy system. Label a different index card for each child in your class. Pick cards from the stack to give each child the opportunity to participate.

Joyce K. McShara—Gr. 3, Putnam Valley, NY

Great job!	You're terrific!	Way to go!	Excellent!	Hurray for you!	You're #1
Great job!	You're terrific!	Way to go!	Excellent!	Hurray for you!	You're #1
Great job!	You're terrific!	Way to go!	Excellent!	Hurray for you!	You're #1
Great job!	You're terrific!	Way to go!	Excellent!	Hurray for you!	You're #1
Great job!	You're terrific!	Way to go!	Excellent!	Hurray for you!	You're #1
Great job!	You're terrific!	Way to go!	Excellent!	Hurray for you!	You're #1
Great job!	You're terrific!	Way to go!	Excellent!	Hurray for you!	You're #1

Patterns

Use with "Penny Power" on page 66.

Cooperative-Learning Sticker Cards

Quickly divide students into cooperative groups of three, four, six, or 12 with this sticker-card system. To make a set of cards, you need 24 index cards and four sets of theme-related stickers.

Example:
Holidays—(six groups of four) 4 Halloween, 4 Christmas, 4 Valentines, 4 St. Patrick's Day, 4 Easter, and 4 Fourth Of July
Color—(eight groups of three) 3 red, 3 yellow, 3 blue, 3 green, 3 purple, 3 pink, 3 orange, and 3 white (smile stickers)
Sports—(four groups of six) 6 baseball, 6 basketball, 6 football, and 6 soccer
Pets—(two groups of 12) 12 cats and 12 dogs

To arrange the stickers, begin with the holiday theme and place one holiday sticker on each card; then mix up the cards. Next place one sports sticker on each card and mix up the cards. Continue in this manner until each card has four different theme stickers. If there are more than 24 students in your class, make a wild card as shown for each extra student.

To utilize the system, give each child a sticker card. To divide your students into four groups of six, call out the sports theme. Students with baseball stickers form one group, those with basketball stickers form another group, and so on. A student who draws a wild card can join the group of her choice. For future group activities, redistribute the cards and choose the theme according to your desired group size. This system ensures easy random grouping every time.

Dawn M. Leahy—Grs. 7–8, St. Germaine School, Oak Lawn, IL

Sing A Song Of Directions

Grab students' attention by singing your directions to the tune of "The More We Get Together." A variety of directions can be used in place of the underlined words.

We're <u>lining up for recess</u>, <u>for recess</u>, <u>for recess</u>
We're <u>lining up for recess</u> as fast as we can
There's (child's name), and (child's name)
There's (child's name), and (child's name)
We're <u>lining up for recess</u> as fast as we can

Regina Walker—Gr. K, Sugar Creek Elementary, Bentonville, AR

We're sitting down for qui - et time, for qui - et time, for qui - et time

Real And Ridiculous Rules!

Creating classroom rules is a great activity for students, but this activity turns rule-making into a totally entertaining experience! Duplicate the rules sheet on page 71. Enlarge the page, if desired. As a group, have students brainstorm a list of sensible rules for your classroom such as:
—Raise your hand before speaking.
—Speak quietly in groups.
—Keep your hands and feet to yourself.

Record your final list of rules on the rules sheet. After completing your list, let the fun begin. Encourage students to think of ridiculous rules such as:
—Don't sit on your head.
—Don't drink water through your ears.

Conclude the activity by having each child illustrate a sensible rule on one side of a sheet of paper and a ridiculous rule on the other side of his paper. Enjoy a few giggles by having students share their illustrations with one another.

Kris Coolican—Gr. 4, St. Anthony Of Padua, Dunmore, PA

Cooperative Little Ants

This discipline program offers tremendous incentive for your youngsters. To prepare, designate one bulletin board for the program. Mount the title and the ant and flower characters to your board. Then mount a sheet of poster board labeled with your classroom rules. Next label a clear plastic cup for each child. Attach the cups in rows to your bulletin board using adhesive Velcro. Duplicate the chart on page 72 for each child and tape the chart to his desk. Then duplicate a supply of ant markers from page 73 and cut them out.

To implement the program, review and discuss the rules with your children. Throughout the day, place ant markers in the students' cups when positive behavior is exhibited. At the end of each day, have each child remove his cup from the board and count his markers. If the child has earned a predetermined number of ant markers, he becomes a member of The Ant Club. Each day that the child becomes a club member, he receives a stamp on his Ant-Club Trail (page 72). Award privileges and small prizes (see page 74 for reproducibles), when the child reaches designated spaces on the trail.

adapted from an idea by Andrea Johnson—Grs. 1–3
Blanton Elementary School, St. Petersburg, FL

Our Classroom Rules

We have discussed the rules we need
to have a positive learning environment.
We agree to:

_____

_____

_____

_____

_____

©The Education Center, Inc. • TEC856

Have An Ant Day!

START

Ants In Your Pants Ribbon

PRIZE #1

Great "Ant" Day Award

10 MINUTES FREE TIME

FINISH

PRIZE #2

Note To Teacher: Use with "Cooperative Little Ants" on page 70.

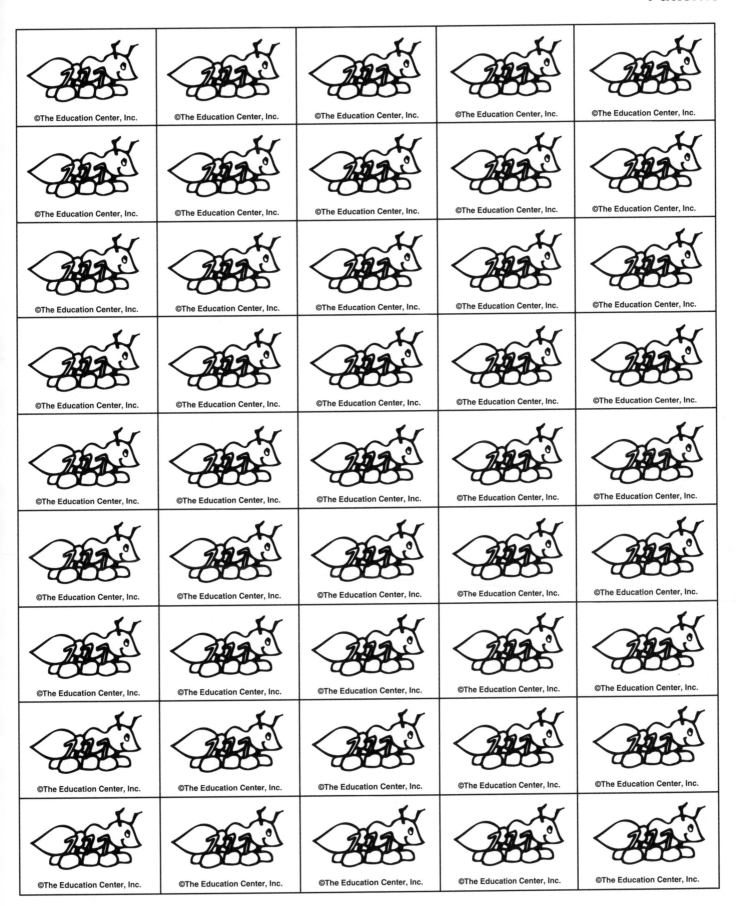

©The Education Center, Inc.

©The Education Center, Inc.

©The Education Center, Inc.

©The Education Center, Inc.

©The Education Center, Inc.

Note To Teacher: Use with "Cooperative Little Ants" on page 70.

Awards

Use with "Cooperative Little Ants" on page 70.

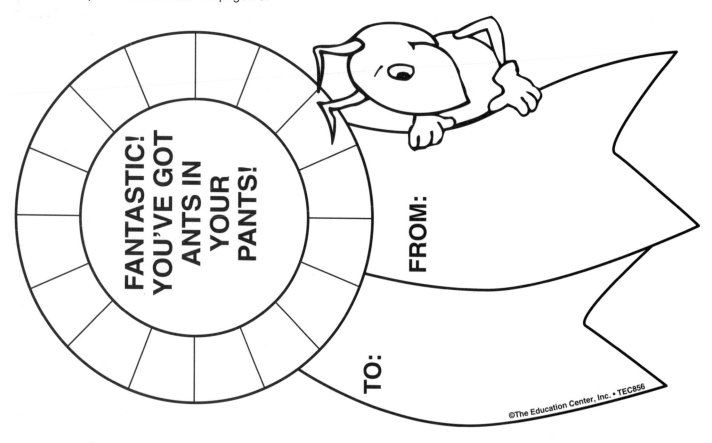

FANTASTIC! YOU'VE GOT ANTS IN YOUR PANTS!

FROM:

TO:

Just to let you know...

HAD A GREAT "ANT" DAY!

ART PROJECTS

Student-Made Stickers

Unique assortments of brightly colored stickers abound with this activity. Provide each of your students with a sheet of 1/2" x 3/4" white labels (available in most office supply stores). Have students create their own sticker designs using fine-tip markers. Using these stickers to reward students is a special treat.

Janice Pfeifer—Gr. 5, East Broad Elementary, Savannah, GA

A Collage Of Me

Here's a great project for the first day of school. Using discarded magazines and newspapers, have students cut out pictures and words that describe themselves. When students have a large assortment of cutouts, have each child glue her cutouts onto a sheet of paper in collage fashion. Have students share their collages with one another, explaining the words and pictures they chose to describe themselves. Display the completed projects for all to see.

Cynthia S. McKinney, Centerville, OH

Who's The Artist?

Generate conversation and critical thinking with this entertaining art project. Begin by having each child make a fingerprint identification card. To make an identification card, give each child a 3" x 5" index card labeled with his name. Using a stamp pad with washable ink, have each child make one fingerprint on his card. Display the fingerprint identification cards and allow time for students to view and discuss them. Then give each child a sheet of white paper. Have each child secretly make several fingerprints on his paper using the same finger used in the identification card. Then have the child use a pen or a pencil to add details to his fingerprints, creating designs, people, or other desired objects. It is important that each child keep his picture a secret. When the pictures are finished, label each picture with a different number and display them around the room. Then have your youngsters compare the pictures to the identification cards to determine each picture's artist.

Barbara Ann Chastain—Gr. 4, Robinson School, Aurora, MO

H is for happy.
U is for useful.
G is for giggling all the time.
O is for outrageous.

Vegetable Wrapping Paper

Students create attractive wrapping paper to use year-round with this fun project. Divide your students into small groups. Give each group a sheet of art paper or a strip of bulletin-board paper. Then provide a bowl of paint and a variety of vegetables—cut into large pieces—for each group. Have each student dip one side of a vegetable in the paint and then press the vegetable on the paper to make a print. Encourage each group of students to cover its paper with an assortment of vegetable prints. Allow the paper to dry; then store the paper for use throughout the year when wrapping gifts.

Diana Boykin, DeZavala Elementary, Midland, TX

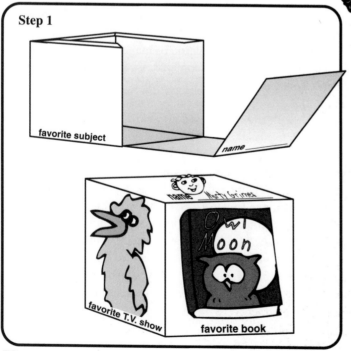

Step 1

favorite subject

name _____

name Marty Grimes

favorite T.V. show

favorite book

Decorative Name Booklets

Students share helpful information about themselves in these colorful booklets. To make booklets, give each child a 5" x 8" piece of white construction paper. Have the child write his name in the center of the paper using a dark crayon. Then using markers, crayons, or watercolors, have the child decorate the entire paper with unusual designs. Have the child glue his paper to the front of a folded 8 1/4" x 12" piece of colored construction paper. Inside the booklet, attach an 8 1/4" x 12" piece of white paper. Have the child write his name vertically as shown. Next to each letter, have the child write something about himself such as "H is for happy." Complete the booklet by having the child write a short paragraph describing his family and his interests. Allow students to share their booklets with one another.

Coletta Preacely Ellis—Grs. 5–6, Wilson Elementary School, Lynwood, CA

Personality Cubes

Duplicate the pattern on page 77 for each of your students. Have each child color the sections of her cube according to each section's label. Then have the child fold on the dotted lines to form a cube as shown in Step 1. Next have the child tape each section in place using transparent tape. Display your students' personality cubes on a table or by suspending them with string.

Julie Eick Granchelli, Warren P. Towne Elementary School, Medina, NY

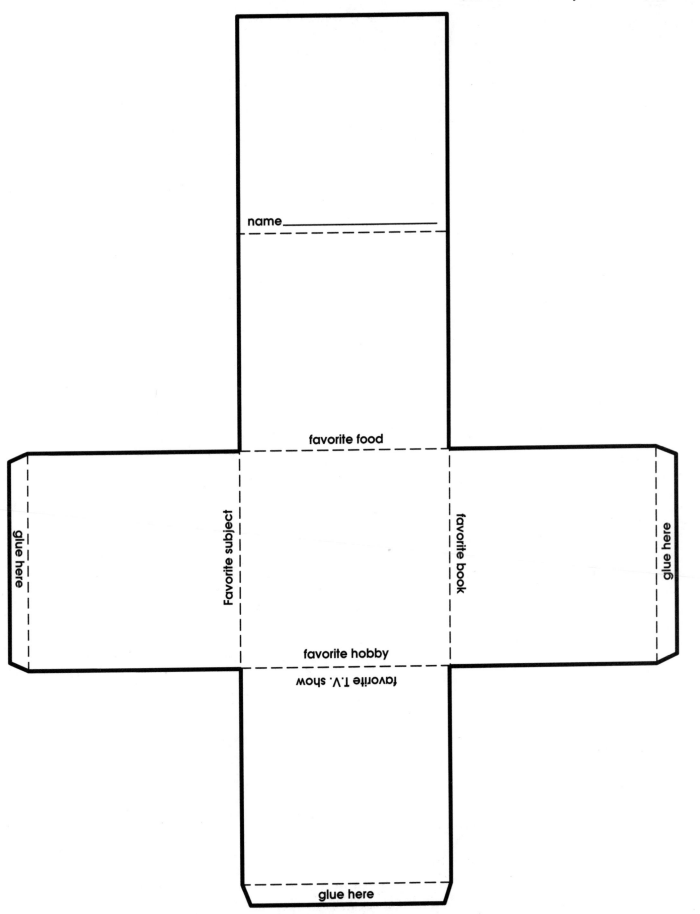

name_____

favorite food

glue here

Favorite subject

favorite book

glue here

favorite hobby

favorite T.V. show

glue here

Steps 1–4

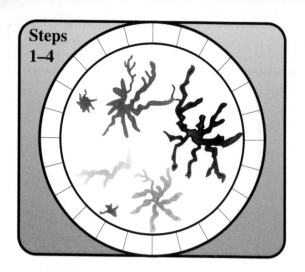

I'm A Work Of Art!

Your students can create this unique art project with ease.

Materials for one project:
9" paper plate
crayons
1 coffee filter
liquid starch
paintbrush
food coloring (various colors)
1 paper clip
masking tape

Step 5

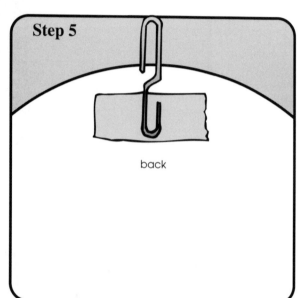

back

Steps:

1. Color the edges of a paper plate as desired.
2. Flatten a coffee filter atop the paper plate.
3. To make the filter stick to the plate, brush a coating of liquid starch over the filter.
4. While the filter is still wet, squeeze three or four drops of food coloring onto the filter. (The colors will spread on the coffee filter.) Allow the project to dry.
5. Tape a paper clip to the back of the paper plate as shown in Step 5.
6. To complete the project, attach a picture of the child in the center of the plate.
7. If desired, display students' artwork on a bulletin board entitled "I'm A Work Of Art!"

adapted from an idea by Andrea Erwin—Gr. K, Bennett Elementary School, Inglewood, CA

Finished project

ONGOING ACTIVITIES

Reading Bubble

Create hours of reading enjoyment and incentive with this easy-to-construct reading environment.

Materials:
1 roll of clear plastic sheeting (found in most hardware stores)
scissors
duct tape
1 box fan

Steps:

1. To construct the bubble area, roll out and cut the plastic sheeting to the desired length.
2. Completely unfold the plastic sheeting; then fold the entire sheet in half.
3. Tape the three open edges closed using duct tape.
4. To connect the fan to the bubble area, cut a three-foot piece of plastic sheeting and tape the two edges together to form a tunnel.
5. Tape one end of the tunnel to the fan as shown in Step 5.
6. Then cut a slit in the narrow end of the bubble and tape the edges of the slit to the opposite side of the tunnel. Gather the plastic as needed.
7. Make an opening in the bubble by cutting an L-shaped slit in the opposite narrow end of the bubble area.
8. Inflate the bubble by turning the fan on high speed. Once the bubble is inflated, turn down the fan speed to medium.

Jill Werbach—Grs. K–5, Bush Elementary School, Fulton, MO

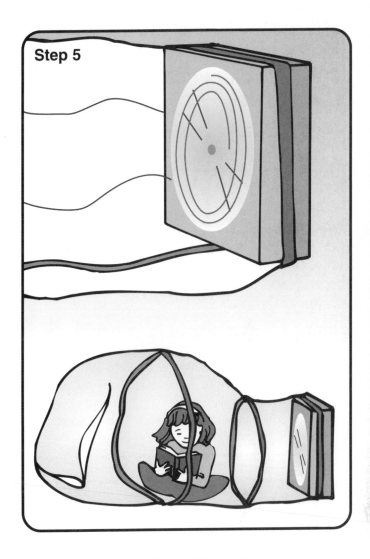

Step 5

Video Fun

During the first week of school, videotape a short interview with each child in your class. Ask each child for information such as her name, age, favorite food, favorite activity, and what she thinks the coming year will be like. Then, at different times during the year, videotape events and highlights of your children. At the end of the year, interview each child on camera once again, asking similar questions to those at the beginning of the year. Show this video presentation on the last day of school for a time of entertainment and memories.

Beth Schimmel—Gr. K, Flagstaff, AZ

Giving Oral Directions

Try this activity at any time during the year for amusing practice with oral directions. Label each of several index cards with tasks such as:
—Make your bed.
—Wash a dog.
—Use a computer.
—Make a sandwich.
—Wash dishes.
—Ride a bike.

To begin, a child draws a card and reads the task silently. Then he gives sequential directions for completing the task without telling what the task is. Students raise their hands when they think they know the described task. Choose another student to draw a task card and continue in the same manner.

Judy Kramer—Gr. 3, High Pointe Elementary, Cedar Hill, TX

Who was your teacher last year?

Mrs. Fin	Mr. Brown	Ms. Moore	Mr. Jones	Other

Spelling Strips

This simple method helps students keep a running list of correctly spelled words. Give each child a 3 1/2" x 8" strip of tagboard labeled with her name. For decoration, place a sticker in the top right corner of each strip. When a child is unsure of a word's spelling, she brings her strip and a pencil to you. Write the word on her strip. Encourage students to write words on the strips themselves, using words they find in their dictionaries.

Kay Beavers—Gr. 2, Grant Elementary School, Willoughby, OH

Picture Graph

Here's an interactive display your students will love. Make a graph on your bulletin board similar to the one shown. Post a question above the graph and label columns with answer choices. Give each child a five-inch square of construction paper. Have each child color a self-portrait on the square. After creating their self-portraits, have students respond to the question above the graph by posting their squares in the appropriate columns. Then discuss the information on the graph. Change the question each week to continue the fun.

Cuqui Gorman—Gr. 4, Quail Hollow Elementary, Tampa, FL

Morgan Hayes

believe
recess
Mississippi
Wednesday
congratulations

Joshua Reynolds

because
their
ruary
er
pe

Shape-Book Stencils

Cookie cutters aren't just for cookies anymore! Use large Wilton's cookie cutters (available in most craft stores) as tracers for your students' shape books. Have students trace and cut out their favorite patterns and then assemble the pages into books. These delightful books are perfect for inspiring great literary works.

Adriana L. García—Gr. 2, Rowan Avenue School, Los Angeles, CA

Daily News

At the beginning of each day, gather your students together to write your news for the day. Have a few students dictate special events and activities. Write the information on a half sheet of chart paper. As an added reinforcement, emphasize the use of capital letters, periods, and quotation marks. Bind your daily news reports with metal rings or shower rings. This collection will be a personal reading favorite with your students.

Heidi L. Hoffman—Gr. 1, Pershing Elementary, Lincoln, NE

Individual Photo Albums

Make personal photo albums for each of your students with this idea. Purchase a small photo album with plastic sleeves for each of your students. (If desired, ask parents to help with the cost of the albums.) Throughout the year, take pictures of your students participating in their daily activities and special events. When developing the pictures, order double prints. Keep one set of prints for yourself and distribute the remaining set among the students' photo albums. Parents will be delighted to receive these books of memories at the end of the school year.

Catherine Pesa, Paul C. Bunn School, Youngstown, OH

Counting Caterpillar

This caterpillar grows and grows with each day of the school year. Duplicate the caterpillar face on page 82 on colored construction paper. Cut out the resulting outline. Then duplicate the body pattern on different colors of construction paper for each day of the school year. Cut out and number the circles consecutively with days of the school year beginning with one. Attach the caterpillar face to your wall. Each day add the next numbered circle to the caterpillar. Children enjoy watching the caterpillar grow throughout the year.

Christine Fischer—Special Education Grs. 4–6, George J. Peters School, Cranston, RI

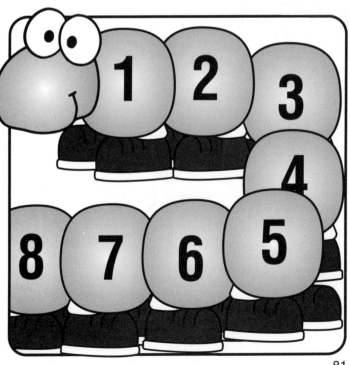

Caterpillar face pattern
Body pattern

Use with "Counting Caterpillar" on page 81.

©The Education Center, Inc.

©The Education Center, Inc.

Note To Teacher: If desired, enlarge the caterpillar patterns to create a larger display.

Help your students understand the concept of by collecting tabs from soft-drink cans. Ask you to estimate how long it will take to collect a million tabs and how much space it will take to store them. Then read aloud the stories *How Much Is A Million?* and *If You Made A Million* by David M. Schwartz. As students bring the tabs to school, store them in resealable plastic bags of 100 tabs each. Using a marker, label the bags as shown. When ten bags of 100 have been collected, pour the contents of the bags into a larger bag labeled 1,000. To increase the number of tabs collected, ask children in other classes to save their tabs for you. You may even want to ask a local newspaper to publish your request for soft-drink tabs. As students begin to grasp the concept of one million, ask students to answer questions such as "Are you in school for a million days each year?" and "How long is a million minutes?" Work together to determine the answers. At the end of the year, donate the tabs to your local recycling center.

Therese Durhman—Gr. 5, Mountain View School, Hickory, NC

A Year In Photos

Create a memory album you'll cherish for years to come. Purchase a photo album with peel-back plastic pages. Photograph each child on the first day of school. Then have each child write a paragraph about herself. Place the photos and the paragraphs in the album. Throughout the year, fill the album with photographs of school activities and field trips. Also include weekly newsletters and school programs. Both students and parents will enjoy this comprehensive record of the school year.

Gloria Small—Grs. 3–4, Washington Island School, Washington Island, WI
Christine Fischer—Special Education Grs. 4–6, George J. Peters School, Cranston, RI

Writing Albums

Store your students' literary works in individual writing albums. Ask each child to purchase a photo album with magnetic pages. Place each child's special stories and illustrations in his album throughout the year. Have students complete their albums at the end of the year by making a dedication page and a table of contents to place in the front of their albums. Your students' parents will be delighted with the resulting memory books.

Cheryl P. Chartrand—Gr. 3, Glenfield Elementary, Lowville, NY

CELEBRATING BIRTHDAYS

Birthday Stories

Give each birthday child a gift he'll cherish with this story-writing project. Attach a sheet of chart paper to your board. At the top of the paper write a cheerful birthday message in bright colors. Then ask students to dictate a story about the birthday child, using only complimentary statements. Discuss the use of capital letters, punctuation marks, quotation marks, and vocabulary words as you write their statements on the chart paper. Display the birthday story throughout the day. Then present the story to the child at the end of the day as a gift.

Heidi Hoffman—Gr. 1, Pershing Elementary, Lincoln, NE

Select A Card

Add excitement to birthday celebrations with this fun activity. Keep a variety of computer-made birthday cards in a special box. On a child's birthday, allow her to choose her own card from the box. Display the card along with an assortment of colored markers. Throughout the day, allow students to color the card and write special messages on it for the birthday child. Periodically, choose a day for a child who has a summer birthday to celebrate an "un-birthday." All students will enjoy their unique cards.

Barbara Ann Chastain—Gr. 4, Robinson School, Aurora, MO

Birthday Basket

Be prepared for your students' birthdays with this basket of goodies. Decorate a basket with lace, ribbon, and bows. Fill the basket with small gifts wrapped in brightly colored paper. On a child's birthday, have her choose a gift to open. Include students with summer birthdays by having them choose gifts on the last day of school.

Debbie Grecco—Gr. 3, Northwest School, Butler, PA

Royalty For A Day

Roll out the red carpet! This idea makes a birthday child feel really special. Construct a simple crown using a strip of bulletin-board border and tape. Have the child wear his crown throughout the day to proclaim this special occasion.

Julie Eick Granchelli, Warren P. Towne Elementary School, Medina, NY

Family Homework Folders

Involve parents in their children's academic progress each week with this great year-round plan. Make a family homework folder for each student by labeling the top and stapling the sides of a manila folder. Each Monday, place the family homework assignment inside each child's folder. The student takes the file home and completes the work with one of her family members. Have the child return her completed work in the folder by the end of the week. Date the outside of the folder as shown, add comments, and attach a sticker to the folder as a reward. Parents will enjoy being actively involved in their children's weekly work. By June, both sides of the folder will be full of stickers and positive comments.

Gloria Bartoloni and Michelle Prentice-Smith—Gr. K, Mabel Paine School, Yorba Linda, CA

First-Day Care Packages For Parents

A child's first day of kindergarten can be an emotional day for his parents, too. To comfort your students' parents, send home special care packages. To make a care package, fill a resealable plastic bag with a tissue, a tea bag, and a cotton ball. Duplicate and cut apart the notes on page 86. Place one note in each bag. Parents are sure to appreciate your thoughtfulness.

Catherine Pesa, Paul C. Bunn School, Youngstown, OH

Parent Visits

Give parents an important role in your class by inviting them to be guest readers. Assign each interested parent a day to bring his favorite children's book to share with the class. The child introduces his parent and may help turn the pages. Not only do the children learn about each other with these visits, but also parents can become better acquainted with the other children in the class.

Deborah Zumbar—Gr. Pre-K, First Presbyterian Preschool, Alliance, OH

Dear Parent,

Thank you for entrusting your child to me. I promise to do my best every day to be your child's companion in learning.

After you have wiped your tears, make yourself a nice warm cup of tea. Put your feet up and relax. Then hold the cotton ball in your hand. The softness will help you to recall the gentle spirit of your child. I will work alongside you this year to help your child grow.

Sincerely,

Dear Parent,

Thank you for entrusting your child to me. I promise to do my best every day to be your child's companion in learning.

After you have wiped your tears, make yourself a nice warm cup of tea. Put your feet up and relax. Then hold the cotton ball in your hand. The softness will help you to recall the gentle spirit of your child. I will work alongside you this year to help your child grow.

Sincerely,

Note To Teacher: Duplicate and cut apart copies of this page to use with "First-Day Care Packages For Parents" on page 85.

Mouse Magnets

Promote parent/teacher communication with these decorative refrigerator magnets.

Materials for one magnet:
28" length of tan macrame jute
tape
scissors
glue gun
2 wiggle eyes
1 small, black pom pom
1 1/2" strip of magnetic tape
1 laminated heart cutout (cut from a 1 1/2" square
    of red construction paper and labeled with the teacher's
    name and phone number)
1 bow cutout (cut from a 1" x 1 1/2" piece of red
    construction paper)

Steps:
1. Fold the strip of jute so that one end of the jute is approximately five inches longer than the other.
2. Form two loops for ears. Before continuing, tape the loops to a flat surface to secure the project. (Step 2)
3. Form the body of the mouse by tying a series of three square knots (Step 3).
4. After tying the third square knot, cut off the loop and the shorter of the two lengths of jute (Step 4).
5. Use a hot glue gun to secure the cut areas in place (Step 5).
6. Using a hot glue gun, glue on wiggle eyes and a pom-pom nose on the front of the mouse. Then glue a strip of magnetic tape to the back of the mouse.
7. Complete the project by gluing the laminated heart to the mouse's body and the bow cutout to the mouse's tail.

Terry Steinke—Pre-K, Emmaus Lutheran School, Indianapolis, IN

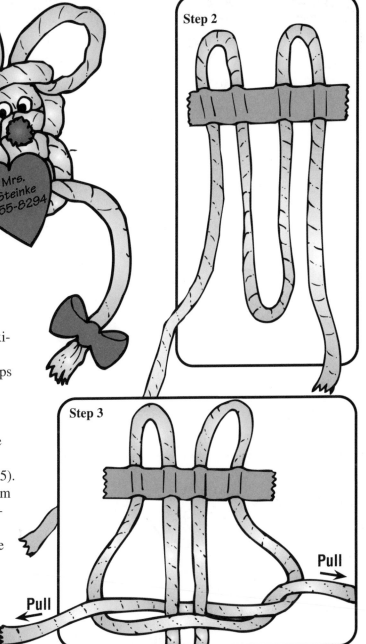

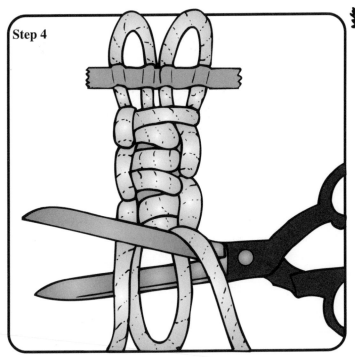

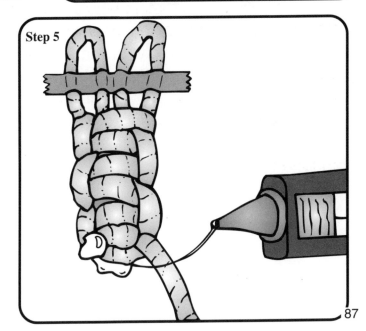

Homework Notebooks

Keep parents informed of students' daily homework with this easy system. Give each child his own personal spiral notebook. Have the child write his daily homework assignments inside the notebook. After completing his homework, the child has his parent sign the notebook beside the assignment.

Debbie Christophersen—Grs. 4–5, North Love Christian School, Rockford, IL

What's The News?

Keep parents in touch with your classroom events with weekly newsletters. Each week, duplicate the open newsletter on page 89. Spend a few minutes each day having students dictate special events and activities. Record their responses on the open newsletter. Allow two students to decorate the newsletter. Name the illustrators before duplicating copies for parents at the end of the week. This keeps the lines of communication open, and the newsletters are nice keepsakes for parents throughout the year.

Karen Cook—Gr. K, McDonough Primary School, McDonough, GA

IEP Follow-Up Notes

Planning a student's Individual Education Plan can be a complex process involving many school professionals, therapists, and outside support agencies. To help parents feel like essential participants in the process, send notes to follow up the meetings. In each note, thank the parent for coming, summarize the plans made in the meeting, and express the important role the parent has in her child's education. These notes not only help express your appreciation, but also reinforce the feeling that a cooperative effort is being made by the school staff to meet a child's special needs.

Karen A. Gilley—Gr. Pre-K, Lake Trafford Elementary, Immokalee, FL

Parent Involvement Display

Invite parents to volunteer in your classroom with an eye-catching display. On your display, post categories such as Field Trips, Parties, and Donating Materials For Projects. Below each category, post a sign-up sheet. Parents will appreciate knowing all of the different ways they can contribute.

Tina Brown—Special Education Grs. 5–6, Van Cortlandtville Elementary School, Mohegan Lake, NY

Our Class Newsletter

month

Teacher: | **Grade:** | **Issue Number:**

Note To Teacher: Use with "What's The News?" on page 88.

Handy Thank-You Notes

Create a supply of thank-you notes with the help of your students. On a sheet of 11" x 17" copy paper, trace each child's hand to make a border. Have each child write her name inside her hand outline. Reduce the design using a copy machine; then duplicate a supply of notes on colored copy paper. Write notes of thanks to special helpers throughout the year on this personalized paper.

Catherine Pesa, Paul C. Bunn School, Youngstown, OH

Star Readers

Encourage parents and children to read together with the Star Readers program. Duplicate a supply of charts from page 91 and give one to each child at the beginning of each week. Each day that a child and his parent read together, they color the star for the appropriate day and write the name of the reading material in the space provided. The child returns his completed chart to school on Friday. After a predetermined number of days of reading, reward students with stickers or bookmarks.

adapted from an idea by Gloria Bartoloni and Michelle Prentice-Smith—Gr. K, Mabel Paine School, Yorba Linda, CA

Parent/Teacher Correspondence

Keep track of your correspondence with parents with this convenient system. Inside a large three-ring binder, place a pocket divider labeled for each child. When parents send notes to school, file them in the appropriate pockets. Write your notes to parents on carbon paper and file the extra copies in students' divider pockets.

Catherine Pesal, Youngstown, OH

Supplies In A Fishbowl

Use a fishbowl on Open House night or conference day to encourage parents to contribute supplies to your classroom. Label each of several fish-shaped cards with a different item such as yarn, a package of construction paper, colored markers, and glue. Place the cards inside the fishbowl. Beside the bowl, display a sign explaining your need for these supplies. If parents decide to contribute, they simply take a card from the fishbowl and then purchase that item for the class.

Lori Wilcox—Gr. 2, Jefferson Elementary, Huntington, NY

Be A Star Reader!

Name _____ Week of _____

Color the star each day that you and your parent read together.
Then write the title of the book in the space provided.

Monday

Tuesday

Wednesday

Thursday

Please return this chart to school on Friday.
Happy Reading!

Note To Teacher: Use with "Star Readers" on page 90.

Traveling Notebooks

Foster communication with parents using this helpful tool. Label a spiral notebook for each child. When it is necessary to send messages of praise or concern or to inform parents of special events, write the messages in the notebooks and have the children take the notebooks home. Encourage parents to use the notebooks to write their own questions and concerns.

Tina Brown—Special Education Grs. 5–6, Van Cortlandtville Elementary School, Mohegan Lake, NY

Parent Information Sheet

Some of your students' parents may have talents, hobbies, or occupations they would like to share with your class. To determine your resources, duplicate the information sheet on page 93 for each parent and send it home during the first week of school. As the sheets are returned, keep a record of the parents who are willing to help out in class and the parents whose interests or occupations can be incorporated into your units.

Sonya Franklin—Gr. 5, Pell City-Kennedy Elementary, Pell City, AL

Calendar Of Events

Keep your students' parents informed with class calendars. Each month duplicate the calendar pattern on page 94. Label the calendar with the dates of activities, birthdays, themes, and special events for that month. Then duplicate the calendar for each of your students' parents. Ask parents to post their calendars in visible places in their homes to keep track of your daily events.

Karen Cook—Gr. K, McDonough Primary School, McDonough, GA

Parent Homework

Involve parents in your thematic units with simple homework assignments. For example, during a unit about nursery rhymes, send home assignment papers asking parents to write the names of their favorite nursery-rhyme characters. When the homework is returned, use the information to create a class graph.

Deb Waghorn, Marcia Boone and Robin Gattis—Gr. K, Seagoville Elementary School, Seagoville, TX

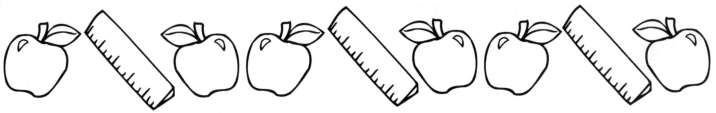

Dear Parent,

You are a valuable part of your child's education. Please take a moment to complete this form about how you would like to be involved this year.

Would you be willing to share your interests or your occupation with us? _____

Hobbies and interests: _____
_____

Occupation: _____

Would you like to assist in class? _____
    If so, how would you like to assist? _____
    _____

Please list your questions and comments below.

_____
_____
_____
_____

Sincerely,

_____

Please return.

Note To Teacher: Use with "Parent Information Sheet" on page 92.

94

Sunday	Monday	Tuesday	Wednesday	Thursday	Friday	Saturday

Note To Teacher: Use with "Calendar Of Events" on page 92.

OPEN HOUSE ACTIVITIES

Class Brochure

Have your youngsters develop class brochures to use as Open House souvenirs. To make a brochure, fold a sheet of white 8 1/2" x 11" paper into three sections as shown in. On the front cover of the brochure, write your school's name, your name, the grade level, and the year. On the back cover list the names of all of your students. Label the inside of the brochure with various events of a typical school day such as library, art, P.E., and computer lab. Have students dictate sentences about each event and write their sentences below each label. On separate pieces of white paper, have students use pencils to draw pictures illustrating these events. When their pictures are complete, display them at the front of the room. Have the students vote which pictures to use in each section of the brochure. Cut out and attach the selected pictures in the appropriate spaces and then duplicate the completed brochure for each child's parent.

Elizabeth A. Main—Gr. 1, Davenport Elementary School, Davenport, FL

Desk Decorations

This unique project results in adorable decorations for Open House. Have each child work with a partner to trace one another's heads and shoulders on tagboard. Then have each child cut out his outline and color both the front and back to look like himself. Encourage students to emphasize features that make them unique such as hair color and glasses. Have each child bring to school one of his T-shirts. Have the child slip the T-shirt over the cutout and then position it over the back of his chair. When parents enter your room at Open House, they will be delighted to see this charming group of children.

Karen Bryant—Gr. 2, Danforth Primary School, Macon, GA

Open House Essays

Invite your students to share personal essays with their parents during Open House. A few days before Open House, ask children to recall their feelings, thoughts, expectations, and activities during the first few days of school. Then have each child write one or two paragraphs describing his recollections. On the evening of Open House, have each child sit with his family members, read his essay to them, and answer any questions they might have. Parents enjoy sharing these experiences with their children.

Tina Brown—Special Education Grs. 5–6, Van Cortlandtville Elementary School, Mohegan Lake, NY

Lights! Camera! Action!

Create an Open House evening that parents will not soon forget by showing a class video. Prior to Open House night, videotape your students participating in their daily activities such as writing in journals, using math manipulatives, playing outside, and eating lunch. Choose individual students to explain such things as your homework policy and class rules on the video. Parents will be entertained as they get a firsthand peek into their children's school activities.

Lori Wilcox—Gr. 2, Jefferson Elementary School, Huntington, NY

Open House Art Displays

Parents enjoy viewing upcoming art projects with these creative displays. Throughout the previous school year, save one of each art project that your students make. Display each project during next year's Open House. Encourage interested parents to contribute materials or their assistance during the year for various projects.

Peggy Sloan—Gr. Pre-K, Oak Forest Park District, Oak Forest, IL

Upcoming Art Projects

Shape Scarecrow

Self-Portrait

Cone Santa

Exotic Eggs

Walnut Turkey

Open House Folders

Present your students' best work in special folders for Open House night. To make a folder, have each child trace the pattern on page 98 on a folded piece of 12" x 18" construction paper. Using crayons or markers, have the child color the outline to look like himself. If desired, provide a mirror for students to use to assist them in adding details to their illustrations. Place the completed folders on each child's desk for Open House and fill the folders with student work for parents to admire.

Pat Gaddis—Gr. Pre-K, Houston, TX

red

"Auto-Biographies"

This motivational writing activity results in great reading material for parents. Ask each student to provide information such as her time of birth, her weight and length, and the weather conditions on the day she was born. Also, have each child bring in one of her recent school photographs. Duplicate the car pattern on page 97 for each of your students. Using the information that they have about themselves, have students write "auto-biographies" on their car patterns. Have students determine how many inches they have grown and how many pounds they have gained since they were born. Then have them write about any other important events in their lives. Have students cut out their cars. Mount the completed "auto-biographies" on a bulletin board. Reading these delightful stories are an Open House treat!

Cindy Sweeney—Gr. 3, Homan Elementary, Schererville, IN

Sneak Preview

Give parents a preview of the year to come with an informative slide show. Throughout this year, take many slides of your children performing various tasks, participating in learning activities, and making projects. Show the slides to your class at the end of this year, but then put the slides to an even better use. Show the slides at next year's Open House to allow parents to see what lies ahead for their children.

Sandra Patane, ABC Preschool, Fulton, NY

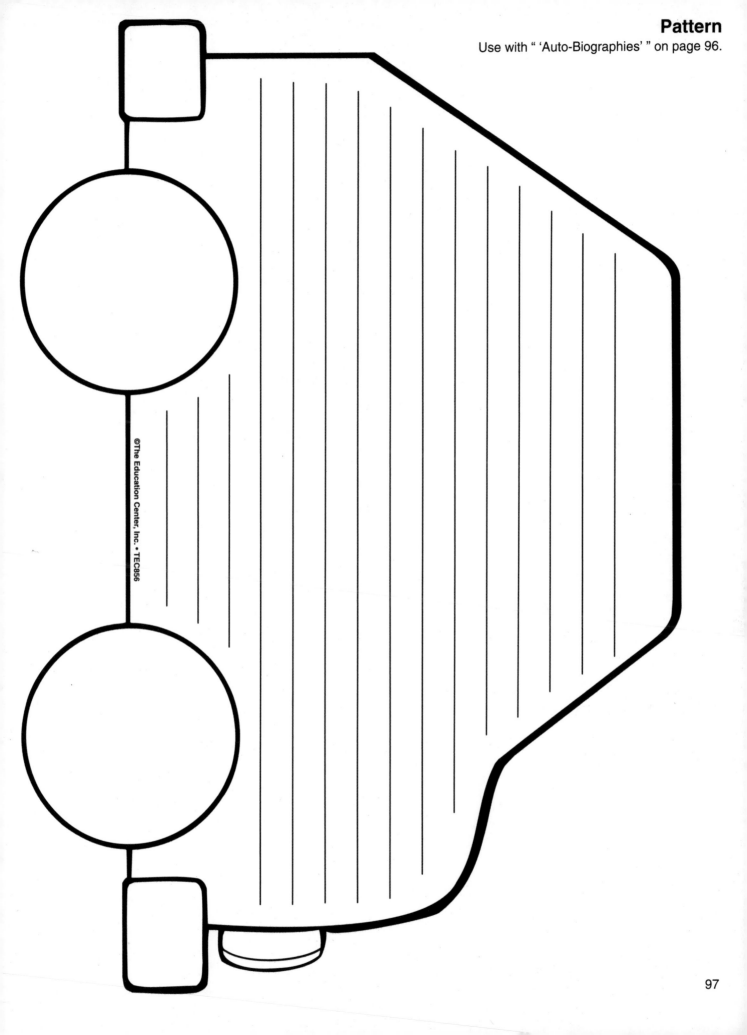

©The Education Center, Inc. • TEC856

Pattern

Use with "Open House Folders" on page 96.

The Importance Of Reading

Open House is a great time to emphasize to parents the importance of reading aloud to their children. To encourage reading, display a variety of great children's literature and invite parents to check them out. You may want to give sneak previews of some of the books to pique parents' interests. Also display a copy of Jim Trelease's *The Read Aloud Handbook* to help parents identify quality literature selections for their children. Encourage parents to utilize the school library to find interesting and entertaining children's books. It won't be long before parents discover the joy of sharing quality literature with their children.

Kathleen Darby—Gr. 1, Community School, Cumberland, RI

Scavenger Hunt

Back-To-School Night is lots of fun with this parent/child activity. Design your own scavenger hunt using the reproducible on page 100. Duplicate the open page and program it with directions such as:

—Have your parent look at the papers on your desk.
—Have your parent read our classroom rules with you.
—Complete the activity at the math center with your parent.
—Introduce your parent to your teacher.
—Visit the school library.
—Visit the computer lab.

Duplicate the desired number of copies. When parents and children arrive, have them take a scavenger-hunt sheet and begin the activities. Your Back-To-School Night will be a great success with this entertaining activity.

Donna Nelson—Gr. K, Mosinee Elementary School, Mosinee, WI
Renee Myers—Gr. K, Snowville School, Hiwassee, VA

Cookie Decorating

Add a tasty twist to your Back-To-School Night with a parent/child cookie-decorating activity. Bake a supply of theme-shaped sugar cookies for your students and their parents. Provide several colors and flavors of frosting, and a variety of utensils. Have students and parents decorate their cookies together for a fun family activity. Yum!

Renee Myers—Gr. K, Snowville School, Hiwassee, VA

Open House Snacks

Make your Open House deliciously special with each family's favorite treat. Before Open House night, ask each child to bring in a simple snack recipe that is her family's favorite. Then prepare the snacks as a class and serve them at Open House as a nice surprise.

Tina Brown—Special Education Grs. 5–6, Van Cortlandtville Elementary School, Mohegan Lake, NY

Prize Attendance

Encourage students and their parents to attend Open House with a gift drawing. Purchase a few small prizes such as stationery or plants for parents and clay or markers for children. Display these items for your students a few days before Open House. Explain to your children that each parent and each child who attends Open House will have a chance to win a prize. Have a drawing for the prizes the day after Open House.

Jane Williams—Gr. 1, Milan Elementary, Grants, NM

Welcome To _____'s

teacher's name

Scavenger Hunt

Follow the directions below. Have fun!

©The Education Center, Inc. • TEC856

Note To Teacher: Use this page with "Scavenger Hunt" on page 99.

ORGANIZING STUDENT MATERIALS

Individual Paint Containers

Use empty 35mm film containers to create convenient paint holders for your students. Contact a local film-developing company to obtain several containers for each student. Fill each container halfway with liquid tempera paint. Leave the caps off the containers until the paint dries. Then cap the containers for storage. To use the paint, the child opens one of his containers, wets the tip of a paintbrush, and brushes the paintbrush across the dried paint. These containers really help minimize messes.

adapted from an idea by Adriana L. García—Gr. 2, Rowan Avenue School, Los Angeles, CA

Lunch-Ticket Storage

Students can easily store their lunch and milk tickets in this handy container. Purchase a plastic, multi-drawer storage container or a tackle box from your local hardware store. Label a drawer for each student. Each day when the child enters the classroom, she places her ticket inside her drawer for safekeeping.

Louis Lessor—Gr. 2, Westside Elementary, Sun Prairie, WI

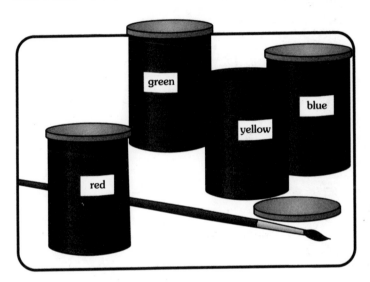

Four-Month Organizer

Students gain organizational skills with this daily system. To create a fall organizer for each child, you need a two-pocket folder, one copy each of pages 102 and 103, clear Con-Tact paper, and a permanent marker. Glue the September/October calendar page to the front of the folder. Then glue the November/December page to the back of the folder. (Color the art on these pages, if desired.) Next, cover the entire folder with clear Con-Tact paper for durability. Using the permanent marker, write the child's name on the front of the folder. Inside the folder, label one pocket *School* and the opposite pocket *Home*.

To use the system, the child places her papers in the Home pocket each day. Her parent removes the papers from this pocket at home. The School pocket is used to hold notes to her teacher or completed homework. Each day the child brings her folder to school, reward her with a sticker on the appropriate day of her calendar. For the five-month spring semester, make new folders for your students using the calendar reproducibles on pages 104 and 105.

Kathy Ploeger, Mason Ridge Elementary School, Creve Coeur, MO

September

October

Name: _____

Note To Teacher: Use with "Four-Month Organizer" on page 101.

November

December

Name: _____

January

February

Name: _____

Note To Teacher: Use with "Four-Month Organizer" on page 101.

March

April

May

Note To Teacher: Use with "Four-Month Organizer" on page 101.

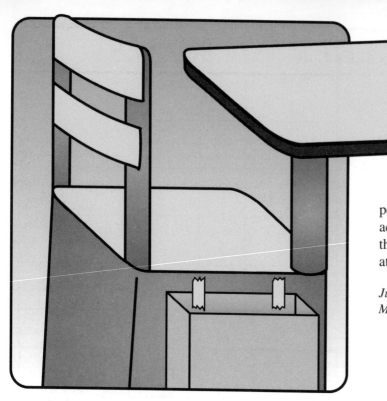

Individual Garbage Bags

Help keep your floors tidy with this great tip. Tape a paper lunch bag to the side of each child's desk. As the child accumulates scraps and other garbage, have him place it in the bag. Have students empty their bags into the trash can at the end of each day.

Julie Eick Granchelli, Warren P. Towne Elementary School, Medina, NY

No More Leaky Glue Caps

Before throwing away empty glue bottles, remove the caps. Wash the caps and store them. Then when a child has a leaky glue-bottle cap, simply throw it away and replace it with one that doesn't leak.

VaReane Gray Heese—Gr. 2, Omaha, NE

Paper Organizers

This timesaving system helps students transport papers to and from school. Give each child a folder with two pockets. Label one pocket *Home* and label the other pocket *School*. As papers and homework assignments are distributed during the day, students place them in the take-home pocket. At home, students place completed assignments and notes from their parents in the give-to-the-teacher pockets. This is an easy way for students to stay organized and reduce the risk of losing important papers.

Alison Taylor—Gr. 4, Wexford Elementary, Wexford, PA

Personal Pouches

To prevent young children from losing important papers, try using special message pouches. To make a message pouch, label a resealable plastic bag with each child's name, room number, and teacher's name. Use a hole puncher to punch two holes at the top of the bag as shown. Then tie a length of yarn or ribbon through the holes. Place papers and messages inside the pouch and hang the pouch around the child's neck to take home.

Gladys Sarmiento—Gr. Pre-K, Pueblo Head Start, Pueblo, CO

Space-Saving Book Display

This great book display is a space saver. To make the display, attach a cup hook below either end of your chalkboard or bulletin board. Position a length of wire between the two cup hooks. Secure the wire by twisting the ends around the hooks, making sure the length of wire is taut. Clip brightly colored plastic clothespins along the wire. Display your favorite books by clipping them to the wire.

Marcella Wise—Gr. 2, St. Edward's School, Seattle, WA

Preprinted Labels

Customize your own message labels with the help of an address-label company. Instead of ordering labels with your name and address printed on them, order labels with messages such as "Please correct and return by _____" or "This book belongs to _____." These labels are attractive time-savers.

Julie Eick Granchelli, Warren P. Towne Elementary School, Medina, NY

Remember For Next Year

How many times have you thought of a great lesson or project idea after it was too late to use it? This tip helps you capture those great ideas to use the following year. Each month, staple a sheet of paper (labeled for that month) in the front of your plan book. When you are reminded of a great idea for a unit or a theme, write the idea on the paper. File each month's idea list in a safe place to use next year.

Julie Eick Granchelli, Medina, NY

Student Numbers

Alphabetize students' papers with ease by using this timesaving system. Beginning with the number one, assign each student—in alphabetical order—his own personal number. Each time students write their names on their papers, they also write their personal numbers. This allows you to quickly sequence students' papers and reduce the time spent recording grades. A brief look through the papers also reveals which students have not yet turned in their assignments.

Joanne Rosengren, Nashotah, WI

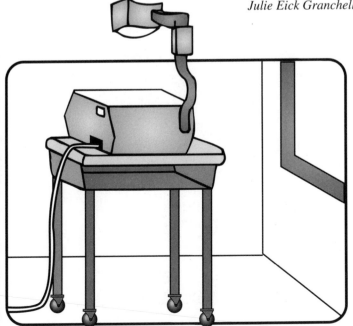

Organization Cart

Attach wheels to the legs of a school desk to create a mobile storage cart for your overhead projector. Place the projector atop the desk and store wipe-off pens, transparencies, and other supplies inside the desk.

Elaine Kraiger, Lilja School, Natick, MA

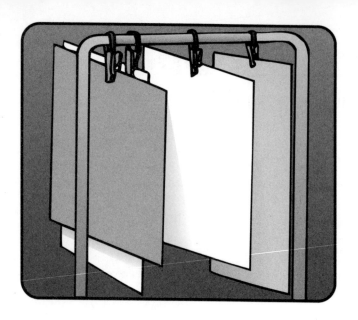

Science-Center Materials

Be on the lookout during the year for interesting items that can be used in your science center. Seashells, fall leaves, unusual rocks, seeds, empty bird nests, and pinecones can all be incorporated into your lessons. So use your vacations, outdoor workdays, or leisurely walks to collect these valuable treasures.

Kathleen Darby—Gr. 1, Community School, Cumberland, RI

Homework Roundup

If you have difficulty keeping track of your students' homework assignments, this is the idea for you. Duplicate several copies of your class roster. Each day have one of your students collect the homework assignments. Then, using a preprinted roster, have that child cross out the names of students who turned in their work. By glancing at this homework roster, you can easily see which students have homework yet to be returned.

Diane Barnfield—Gr. 6, Puxico Elementary, Puxico, MO

Teacher's Apron

When you're teaching, the materials you need never seem to be in the proper location at the proper time. Remedy this problem with a simple solution. Purchase a carpenter's apron from a local hardware store. Use fabric paint to add your own personal touches. Then fill the pockets of the apron with useful items such as markers, pencils, grading stamps, and paper. Everything you need is at your fingertips!

Adriana L. García—Gr. 2, Rowan Avenue School, Los Angeles, CA

Chart Storage

Conveniently store all of your charts and posters with this great storage rack. To make a storage rack, you will need an upright metal stand (such as a flip-chart stand), string, and a supply of plastic clothespins with small holes in the ends. Insert a length of string through both holes of a clothespin. Tie the string to the top bar of the rack. Clip a chart to the clothespin and...voila! You have instant storage.

Debbie Christophersen—Grs. 4–5, North Love Christian School, Rockford, IL

Uses For Die-Cut Patterns

Die-cut machines help make a variety of convenient items for your classroom. Here's a list of suggestions.
—Staple patterns around your bulletin board to create a thematic border.
—Label theme-related patterns appropriately to create task cards.
—Label a set of patterns with math facts to use as flash cards.
—Write messages on the patterns to send to parents and faculty members.
—Write notes of praise on patterns to give as awards.
—Write each child's name on a pattern to wear as a nametag.
—Cut patterns in half and program the halves with items to match.
—Program the patterns with items to match and place them facedown to use in a memory game.
—Use seasonal patterns as gift tags.

Andrea Johnson—Grs. 1–3, Blanton Elementary, St. Petersburg, FL

Oh, Those Delicious Apples!

What better way to begin the year than with an apple thematic unit. Your students will enjoy these entertaining and tasty activities.

ideas contributed by
Catherine Pesa, Paul C. Bunn School, Youngstown, OH
Jenny Zollers—Gr. 1, Kenilworth Elementary School, Bowie, MD

Informative Nametags

Students reveal a wealth of personal information with these symbolic nametags. Using the pattern on page 111, duplicate the apple nametag on white construction paper for each of your students. Have each child cut out his nametag and write his name and school on the lines provided. Then display a color code as shown for students to use when coloring their nametags. For example, a boy colors only one leaf green and a girl colors both leaves green. Bus riders color the worm purple and other students color the worm blue. Students who own pets color the stem brown, while students who do not own pets color the stem yellow. The entire apple is colored with each child's favorite color. Each child who can recite his phone number receives a sticker on his apple.

When students have finished coloring their nametags, gather them together. Then have each child display his nametag. Ask other students to use the color code to decode the information on the nametag.

Apple Cookbooks

Incorporate tasty apple recipes into your thematic apple unit. Have students bring apple recipes from home for dishes such as applesauce, candied apples, baked apples, and apple cider. Make several copies of the reproducible on page 111 and copy the recipes onto the pages. Then duplicate several copies of each page to staple into booklets. Have students make the recipes and wrap individual portions of the recipes in plastic wrap. Sell the apple treats and cookbooks at a bake sale to fund your future cooking projects.

Apple Smiles

Your students will enjoy making these cheerfully tasty treats. To make an apple smile, each child needs two red apple slices, peanut butter, a plastic knife, and four minimarshmallows. First the child spreads peanut butter on one side of each apple slice. Then she places the marshmallows on the peanut butter on one of the slices. She then places the remaining slice (peanut-butter side down) atop the marshmallows. These smiling treats are adorable and nutritious.

I Am Special

This creative-writing/art project makes a nice beginning-of-the-year bulletin board or wall display. Duplicate page 112 on red or green construction paper for each of your students. Also duplicate the reproducible apple card below for each child. Have each child color the letters, the worm, the leaf, and the stem on her apple. Then have the child write her name on the line provided. Next have the child cut out the apple on the outer bold lines. Have the child cut on the dotted lines and fold back on the bold lines so that the flaps fold open as shown. On the reproducible apple card, have the child write the qualities and characteristics that make her unique. Have her cut out the card on the outer bold line. Have the child squeeze a trail of glue outside the apple border. Then have the child position the apple cutout atop the apple card, aligning the apple border with the inside of the window cutout. Display each child's project on a large apple-tree cutout on your bulletin board or wall.

Reproducible Apple Card

©The Education Center, Inc. • TEC856

Use with "Apple Cookbooks" on page 109.

©The Education Center, Inc. • TEC856

Pattern
Use with "I Am Special" on page 110.

I Am
Unique

by _____

Pigs, Pigs, And More Pigs

Begin the school year with a familiar theme. Students will enjoy these activities based on *The Three Little Pigs*.

ideas contributed by
Karen Cook—Gr. K, McDonough Primary School, McDonough, GA
Judi Tuskowski—Gr. 2, Madison Elementary, Stevens Point, WI

Little Pig, Little Pig, Let Me In!

Welcome new students to your classroom through a brick-house door decoration. Design, color, and cut out a brick house using bulletin-board paper. Attach the house around the outside of your door. Mount a class title on the door.

Design A House

As students enter the classroom, allow them to begin coloring a straw, stick, or brick house. Provide several large cardboard boxes and an assortment of crayons or markers. Allow students to work together or separately to create little pig houses. This is a great opening activity, and it occupies students who are having difficulty leaving their parents.

Pig Plays

Read aloud *The Three Little Pigs* to your students. Encourage students to observe the illustrations in the story. Then have students make props to use in class plays. Assign groups of students to design the different types of houses. Assign other groups of children to make costumes. Have different groups of students practice performing their own versions of the play. At the end of the week, have students perform their plays for their classmates.

Piggy Literature

After reading the original version of *The Three Little Pigs*, read aloud Jon Scieszka's *The True Story Of The Three Little Pigs*. Have students identify the differences and similarities between the two stories. Then ask students to decide which version they believe is true.

Piggy-Bank Plan

Reinforce money skills as you implement this "pig-errific" behavior plan. Begin by having each child make a piggy bank from a plastic gallon jug (rinsed and dried). Have each child cut out pig facial features and other decorations from construction paper and glue them to the outside of the jug. Have students display their piggy banks atop their desks. As appropriate behaviors are observed, place plastic or paper coins (see the coin reproducible on page 115) in the students' banks. At the end of each week, have students cash in their coins and enter the number of coins they have in bank books. To make a bank book, simply staple together several sheets of paper. (Designate a page for each coin value.) The child then makes a tally mark or a coin-stamp mark on the appropriate page of the bank book to represent each coin he has. Post a list of prizes and privileges that students can buy with their earned money. Designate a time when students can purchase these items. Have children cross out the coins used in their bank books after each purchase.

• First in line	20¢
• Chew gum for a	15¢
• Move desk by a	10¢
• Sit at the front of the	15¢
• Do 1/2 of homework	
• 10 min	

Let's Pig Out!

Every youngster's mouth will water for the taste of "pigs in a blanket." To make this tasty treat, wrap Vienna sausages in premixed, refrigerated biscuit dough and bake according to the package directions. Yum!

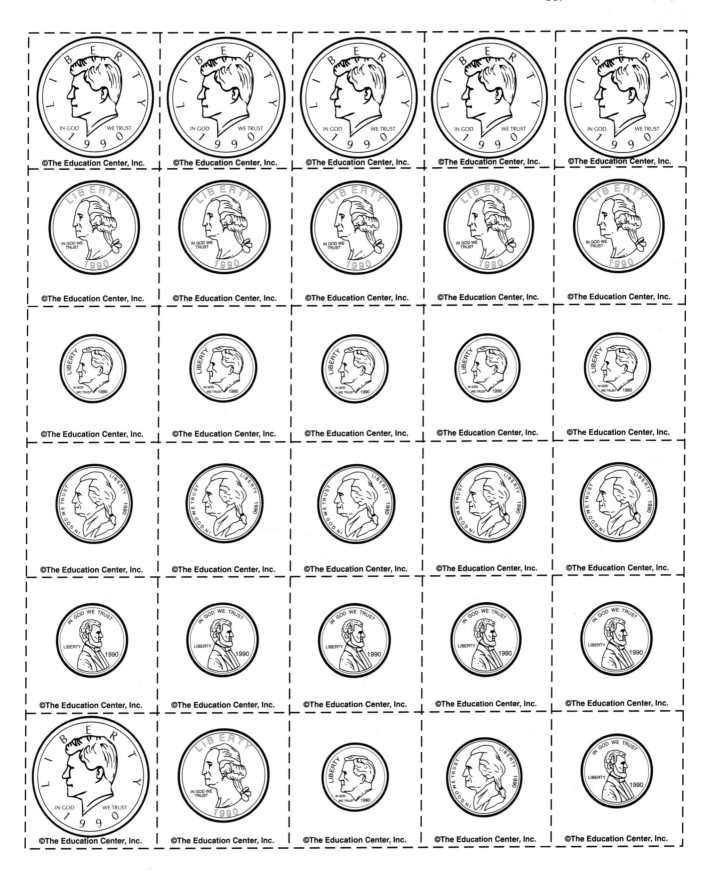

Shoes

ideas by
Christine Maszka—Gr. 2, St. Paul Of The Cross School, Park Ridge, IL

Shoes On Parade

Using the pattern on page 118, have each child trace a shoe onto a sheet of white construction paper. Then have each child cut out her shoe and decorate it using crayons or markers. Display the shoes on a bulletin board.

Math From The Sole

The designs on the soles of shoes provide an interesting lesson about patterns and geometric shapes. To begin the activity, each child needs a sheet of paper and a crayon. Have each child either remove her shoe or sit in a position where she can reach the bottom of her shoe. Then have the child place the paper over the sole of her shoe and use a crayon to make a rubbing of the sole's pattern. Display the rubbings and encourage the children to compare and contrast the shapes and patterns.

Favorite Footwear

Using discarded magazines and catalogs, have students cut out different styles of shoes. Allow students to share their shoe cutouts with their classmates. Then choose one picture of each style of shoe to display on a class graph as shown. Have your youngsters choose their favorite shoe styles and graph their responses.

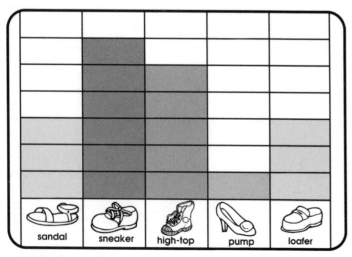

sandal	sneaker	high-top	pump	loafer

Footwear Fantasies

Encourage your children to imagine outrageous shoe adventures. As a class, brainstorm a variety of unusual shoe events and situations. Provide a few story titles such as the titles listed below and have each child write his own shoe story.

—"The Case Of The Missing Sneakers"
—"The Flying Shoes"
—"Incredible Magic Shoes"

After completing their stories, have students make individual books. For each child, duplicate two copies of the shoe pattern on page 118 on construction paper for a cover and duplicate copies of the shoe writing paper on page 119. Have each child cut out the cover pages and the writing pages and copy her story onto the writing pages. Secure the cover and the story pages with staples and have the child decorate the cover of her book. For an added touch, have each child glue a yarn bow to the cover for a shoelace.

Shoes Around The World

Your youngsters can expand their knowledge of other countries by learning about the shoes people wear in different locations. After finding several books with sections explaining types of shoes in different countries, read to your children about a different country's shoe each day. Have students identify each country on a map or a globe. Extend the activity by having groups of students research different countries and write short reports.

Parent Participation

Involve parents in your unit on shoes during your Open House. Have each parent write down her favorite kind of shoe on a slip of paper. On the day after Open House, have students create a graph to show the results. Then have students compare the parent graph to their own class graph and discuss the similarities and differences.

Bookmarks

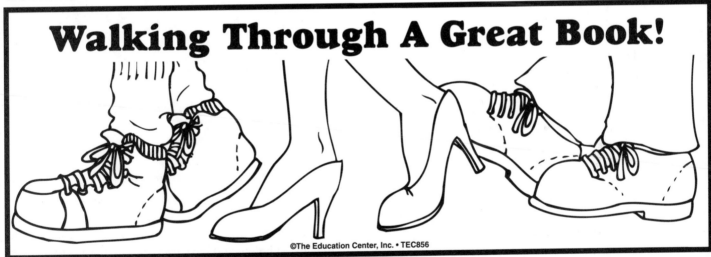

Walking Through A Great Book!

©The Education Center, Inc. • TEC856

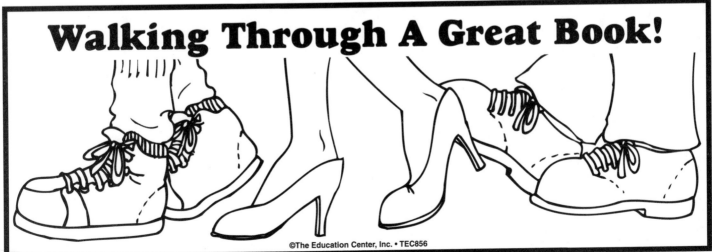

Walking Through A Great Book!

©The Education Center, Inc. • TEC856

Pattern

Use with "Shoes On Parade" and "Footwear Fantasies" on page 116.

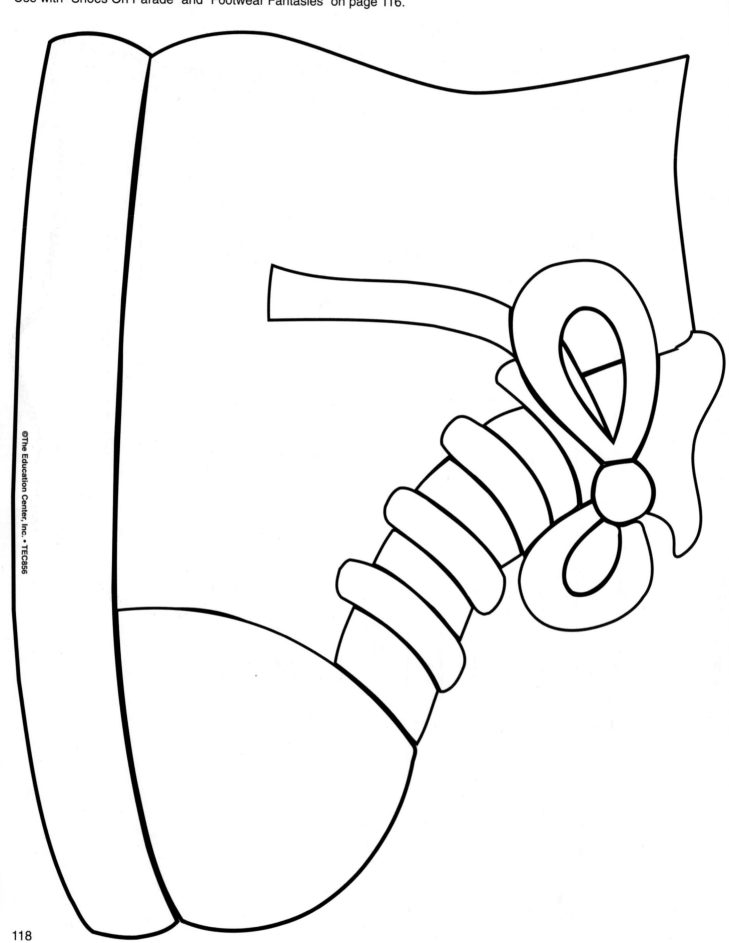

©The Education Center, Inc. • TEC856

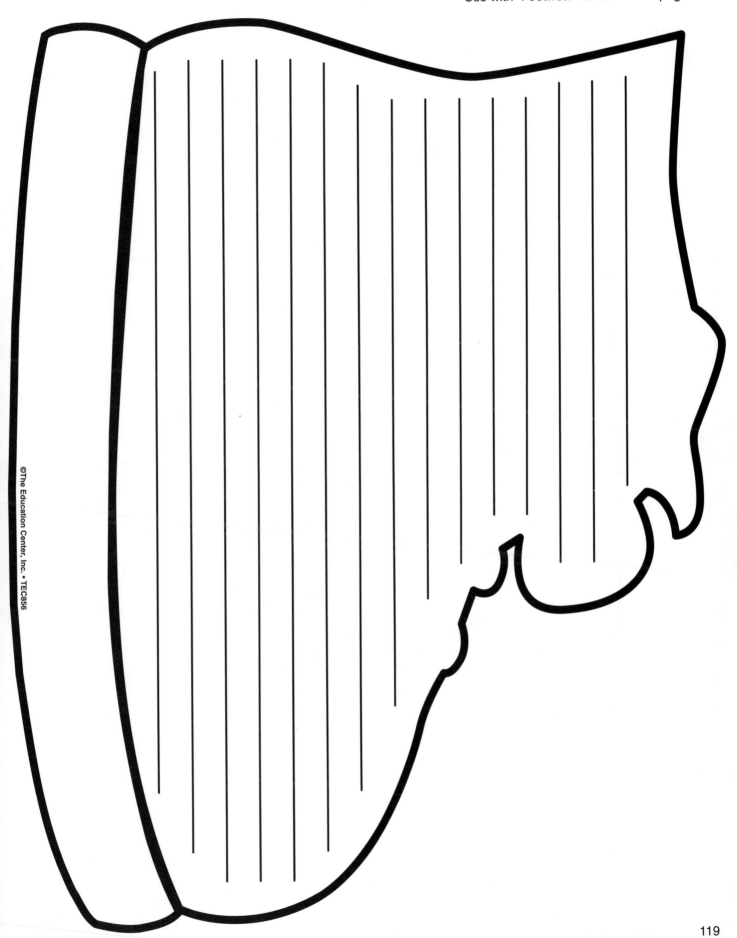

One Last Day At The Beach

Say good-bye to summer with an imaginary day at the beach. On this special day, have students come to school dressed in beach attire such as shorts, Hawaiian shirts, sandals, sunglasses, and beach towels. Then get ready—it's time to hit the beach!

ideas contributed by
Dawn Kelly—Gr. 2, Seminary Attendance Center, Seminary, MS

Ocean Display Background

Create an attractive ocean background on your bulletin board. Staple sheets of aluminum foil to cover the board. Then cut out pastel crepe-paper sheets in varying sizes. Roll up the crepe paper lengthwise to create seaweed. Staple the ends of each seaweed length to the bulletin board. If desired, mount a fishnet on a portion of the bulletin board for an added touch.

A Sea Of Words

Add to your ocean bulletin board with this group activity. Have students brainstorm words they associate with the ocean such as fish, seashells, water, and swimming. Write their words on strips of construction paper and staple them in various places on the bulletin board. Entitle the display "Let's Learn A Sea Of Words."

Ocean Creatures

No ocean is complete without a variety of aquatic creatures. The following projects can be made by students and attached to your bulletin board or suspended from your ceiling.

Starfish And Seashells: Have students make starfish and seashells by tracing the patterns on page 122 on construction paper. Then have students cut out their outlines. Provide dried cereal, glitter, sequins, and other desired materials for students to glue onto their cutouts. Attach the completed projects to your display after the glue is dry.

3-D Creatures: The final touch to your display comes from stuffed ocean animals. To make a stuffed creature, cut out the desired shape from colored bulletin-board paper. Then trace the shape onto another sheet of bulletin-board paper and cut out the shape. Glue the edges of the two outlines together, leaving a three-inch opening for stuffing the creature. Using bulletin-board paper scraps, glue decorations to both sides of the creature. When the glue is dry, stuff the creature with plastic bags. Glue the open edges closed and mount the creature to the ocean display.

Sandbox Writing

This novel activity helps students practice vocabulary or spelling words. Fill a plastic dishpan with sand. Then have two students work together at the sandbox. To practice vocabulary words, one student writes a word in the sand and her partner reads the word. To practice spelling words, one student says a spelling word and her partner writes the word in the sand. Students take turns in this manner as time allows.

Beach-Front Reading

In a corner of your room, position a large beach umbrella, a few lawn chairs, beach towels, sun visors, and other beach items. Add a small child's swimming pool filled with theme-related books. Throughout the day allow students to lounge on the beach, reading good books.

Swimming In Sequence

Practicing ABC order skills is fun with this fishy activity. Duplicate several copies of the fish pattern on page 123 on construction paper. Cut out the fish and label each one with a different word. Code the backs of the cards for self-checking, if desired. Then place the fish in a fishbowl. To play, have students remove the fish from the fishbowl and place the fish in ABC order.

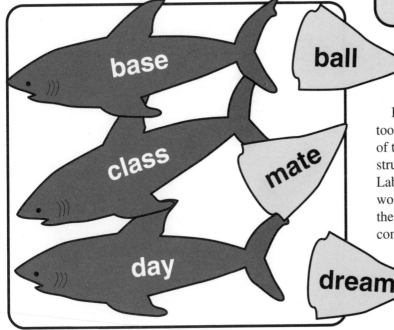

It's A Shark!

In this center activity, students match shark and shark-tooth cutouts to make compound words. Duplicate copies of the shark and shark-tooth patterns on page 123 on construction paper. Cut out the patterns along the outer edges. Label each shark cutout with the first part of a compound word. Then label each shark tooth with the second part of the compound word. Students match the pieces to create compound words.

Patterns

Use with "Ocean Creatures" on page 120.

©The Education Center, Inc.

©The Education Center, Inc.

©The Education Center, Inc.

Pattern

Use with "Swimming In Sequence" on page 121.

©The Education Center, Inc.

Patterns

Use with "It's A Shark!" on page 121.

©The Education Center, Inc. • TEC856

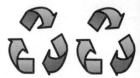

Recycling Resources

Your youngsters will find that taking care of the environment is important and fun with this miniunit.

ideas by
Beth Schimmel, Gr. K, Flagstaff, AZ

You Can Make A Difference!

This bulletin-board display shows children how they can help the environment by recycling. Display a large map of your city and mark the locations of recycling plants or bins. Be sure to identify the kinds of materials that are collected or recycled at each location. Then have students identify the locations that are nearest to their homes and school.

A Wealth Of Information

Provide your students with a variety of literature and resource books dealing with environmental issues and recycling. Encourage students to read both fictional and nonfictional materials and to share new information with their classmates. The fictional books listed below are sure to provide your children with thought-provoking reading pleasure.
—*Farewell To Shady Glade* by Bill Peet (Houghton Mifflin Company, 1966)
—*Just A Dream* by Chris Van Allsburg (Houghton Mifflin Company, 1990)
—*The Lorax* by Dr. Seuss (Random House, 1971)
—*The Paper Bag Prince* by Colin Thompson (Alfred A. Knopf, 1992)
—*The Wump World* by Bill Peet (Houghton Mifflin Company, 1981)

Creativity Corner

Let your students' creative juices flow by making recycled art projects. Designate an art corner in your classroom. Then have students donate a variety of discarded items from home such as plastic milk jugs, paper-towel rolls, magazines, and wrapping paper. Direct students in making various projects or allow students to design and make their own creations in their free time.

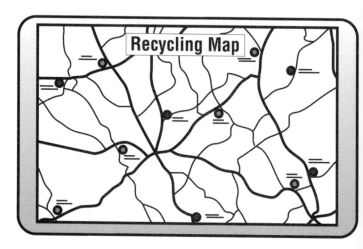

Let's Pitch In!

Demonstrate to your students how simple it is to collect recycled materials. For a designated time, encourage students to bring recyclable materials to school to be placed in bags labeled for various items such as aluminum cans, newspapers, and plastics. Periodically take the items to your local recycling plant. Some plants offer money for certain items, so save this money and use it to improve the environment by purchasing flowers or trees to plant on your school grounds.

Hopping Into A Great Year Welcome!

To: _____

From: _____

Boy, Oh Boy, What A Bookworm!

Keep up the good work!

To: _____

From: _____

Date: _____

"Bee-utiful" Job!

Your writing is delightful.

Here's why: _____

_____

_____

To: _____

From: _____

Stellar Speller Award

I'm proud of

_____
child's name

because _____

_____

_____

_____

From:_____

Date:_____

I'm Not "Lion"!

_____'s

math skills add
up to success.
Good job.

From:_____
Date:_____

HATS OFF TO

_____
child's name

FOR TERRIFIC
BEHAVIOR!

From:_____
Date:_____

Be Prepared!

The first week of school can be very hectic, so treat yourself to a week of hassle-free dinners. Several weeks before school begins, cook and freeze an assortment of tasty recipes. During the first week of school, simply thaw and warm your evening meals and give yourself time to relax!

Kathleen Darby—Gr. 1, Community School, Cumberland, RI

Chill-Out Pie

Beat the back-to-school heat with a cool treat your entire staff will enjoy.

Ingredients:

1 stick of margarine, melted
20-oz. package of Oreo cookies
1/2 gallon of ice cream or frozen yogurt (any flavor)
1 large container of non-dairy whipped topping

Directions:

1. In a large mixing bowl, crush the Oreo cookies and mix them with the melted margarine.
2. Press the Oreo mixture into the bottom of a 9" x 13" pan to form a crust.
3. Spread slightly softened ice cream or yogurt over the crust.
4. Top the ice cream or yogurt with a layer of non-dairy whipped topping.
5. Freeze the dessert until it is ready to serve.
6. Before cutting the pie into pieces, let it stand at room temperature for five to ten minutes.
7. If desired, garnish the pie with chocolate syrup, strawberries, or cherries.

Christine J. Maszka—Gr. 2, St. Paul Of The Cross School, Park Ridge, IL

Friendship Mix

This sweet treat is tasty and easy to make. Simply mix an assortment of peanuts, raisins, and M&M's. Pour the mix into a large bowl to place in your faculty lounge or fill small jars with this sweet mix to present to your colleagues as tokens of your friendship.

Christine J. Maszka, Park Ridge, IL

Help Yourself!

Laugh, Laugh, Laugh!

When your class is showing signs of stress after a test or a long study period, take a joke break. Invite students to share preapproved jokes of their own or read some out of a joke book. You and your students are sure to benefit from these humorous moments.

Barbara Ann Chastain—Gr. 4, Robinson School, Aurora, MO

Journal Time

Make journal time a special time for you. Purchase a decorative journal for the school year. During your students' daily journal-writing sessions, record your highlights and joys as well as your struggles and frustrations. Recording your teaching experiences is a great outlet!

Beth Schimmel—Gr. K, Flagstaff, AZ

Treat The Teacher!

Here's an activity you'll really enjoy. Prepare a reward jar just for you. In the jar, place slips of paper labeled with rewards such as:

— Ten minutes of quiet time in the classroom.
— Choose a student to read a story to the class.
— Students clean their desks.
— Students sing a special song to you.

When students are proud of your accomplishments, allow a child to choose a slip from the jar. Your children then reward you by performing the task on the slip!

Beth Schimmel, Flagstaff, AZ